D1605982

RAMBLES

IN THE

MAMMOTH CAVE

DURING THE YEAR 1844,

BY A VISITER

Alexander Clark Bullitt

With a New Introduction by Harold Meloy

CAVE BOOKS
ST. LOUIS
1985

First edition printed by Morton & Griswold, Louisville, Kentucky, 1845.
First reprint edition printed by Johnson Reprint Corporation,
   New York, New York, 1973.
Second reprint edition printed by Cave Books, St. Louis, Missouri,
   1985.

Library of Congress Cataloging in Publication Data

Bullitt, Alexander Clark, 1807-1868.
   Rambles in the Mammoth Cave, during the year 1844.

   Reprint. Originally published: Louisville: Morton &
Griswold, 1845, With new introd.
   Bibliography: p.
   1. Mammoth Cave (Ky.). 2. Bullitt, Alexander Clark,
1807-1868. I. Title.
F457.M2B9   1985   976.9'75403   85-6698
ISBN 0-939748-16-9 (pbk.)

Cave Books, 756 Harvard Avenue, St. Louis, MO 63130 USA.

Mammoth Cave has inspired hundreds of writers to describe its wonders, generations of scientists to probe its mysteries, and millions of visitors to enjoy its underground grandeur. Exceedingly rich in folklore, history, and legend, the cave has stirred the imagination of Americans for many years.

White men came to Mammoth Cave during the 1790's to dig for saltpetre, which they used to make gunpowder. The first explorers in the region had depended on powder brought over the mountains from the east, but this often proved unsatisfactory, and was too expensive. Pioneers were soon making their own gunpowder. They obtained nitrates by leaching the saltpetre found in the nitrous earth in the cave, and by mixing the nitrates thus obtained with sulphur and charcoal, they produced a dependable grade of powder. Saltpetre mining operations greatly increased during the War of 1812, when 70 workers were employed in the cave, and many tons of nitrate crystals were wagoned to the powder mills in the east.

In his youth, Ebenezer Meriam (1794–1864) played a very active and lucrative role in the saltpetre recovery operations. He was later to become the "highly scientific gentleman of New York" quoted on page 25. At the termination of the war with Britain, saltpetre mining ceased in Mammoth Cave, and Meriam moved on to other pursuits. His fondness for Mammoth Cave remained with him during his highly successful business and scientific career. From his collections of Mammoth Cave literature and his own observations in the cave he wrote in the *New York Municipal Gazette* one of the Mammoth Cave descriptions from which the fabric of *Rambles in the Mammoth Cave during the year 1844* was woven.

Legends and traditions kept pace with history at the cave. The story of the two mummies and Mr. Ward (pp. 23–24) was based partly on fact, and was embellished by early guides to make a good story for visiting tourists. This story, as narrated in *Rambles*, was told to Alexander Bullitt when he visited the cave in 1844 gathering materials for the book.

Nahum Ward (1785–1860), a native of Shrewsbury, Massachusetts, stepped into Mammoth Cave history in the fall of 1815. Two years before, the saltpetre miners had found Indian mummies in nearby Short Cave. One of the mummies was moved to Mammoth Cave for exhibition in the "Haunted Chambers," later called Gothic Avenue. In October 1815, Ward made an 18-hour tour through the cave, where he saw the mummy. On his departure he took the mummy with him. Thereafter he wrote and published a long descriptive account of the cave and of *his* discovery of the mummy. Ward's narrative had instant reader appeal. It was published and republished in whole or in part in numerous newspapers, magazines, and books throughout the country. It appeared in England in 1817 and was republished there again in 1823. Ward and the mummy made Mammoth Cave famous on both sides of the Atlantic.

The parade of visitors to Mammoth Cave began around 1810. After Ward's publications they increased in numbers, and by the 1820's they were coming from England as well. William N. Blane journeyed to Kentucky and was conducted through the cave by Archibald Miller, the former superintendent of the saltpetre operations. Upon his return to England, he wrote a book describing the United States and the cave. Blane's book was published in London in 1824 and again in 1828.

London attorney Godfrey T. Vigne visited Mammoth Cave in July 1831. His book was published the following year in London and described parts of the cave that Blane had not mentioned. Readers in England were thus as well informed about the cave as those in America.

By 1834 enthusiastic American journalists were reporting the cave to be 20 miles long. Within a year, the first instrument survey within the cave was completed. Edmund F. Lee, a civil engineer, spent four months during the winter of 1834–1835 measuring every passage and branch known at

the time. He found the cave to be only a little over
two and a quarter miles in length, and the "length
of all the branches of the cave, taken together,
about eight miles."

After Lee finished his survey, he prepared a
beautiful scale map of the cave and published a
30-page guidebook entitled *Notes on the Mammoth Cave*. Three years later the guidebook became obsolete after Bottomless Pit was crossed,
for beyond Bottomless Pit the guides found miles
of virgin passages, which more than doubled the
total length known to Lee. Lee's little guidebook
was obsolete perhaps, but not discarded, for parts
of it were to appear again in the pages of *Rambles*.

One of the literary lights of the period who became enamoured with Mammoth Cave was Dr.
Robert Montgomery Bird (1805–1854). Practis-
ing physician, professor of Materia Medica and
Institutes of Medicine in Pennsylvania Medical
College, novelist, and playwright, Bird first visited the cave in June of 1833 (not 1832 as reported on page 47). He was delighted with it.
After reading Lee's 1835 guidebook, Dr. Bird
again visited the cave in 1836, and therafter
wrote one of the classics of Mammoth Cave literature. Like Lee, he could describe only less than
one-sixth of the cave now known, and his prose,
like Lee's, is copied again and again throughout
Rambles.

Natural scientists made pilgrimages to the cave.
Dr. John Locke (1792–1856) of the Medical Col-

lege of Ohio in Cincinnati, one of the foremost
geologists in the country, felt compelled to visit
and to study the cave. Many scientists since then
have felt the same compulsion. Locke could not
accept the vertical distances within the cave as
reported by Lee, and he made barometrical measurements of the lower levels in the cave (pp. 86–
87). We know now that Locke was correct,
although Lee's woefully erroneous measurements
of depths made a far better story for the former
guides to tell the visiting public.

On his return to Cincinnati, Dr. Locke gave lec-
tures on the cave in 1842. It is said that these were
published, but diligent search has failed to locate
them. Locke later wrote John Croghan that he
did not have the necessary funds to obtain engravings of his illustrations for the book about the cave
which he had planned to publish.

But others had the financial resources, and publish they did. Even those who had not visited the
cave did not hesitate to write about it. New York
authoress Lydia Maria Child (1802–1880) was
fascinated when one of her friends, who had recently visited the cave, described it for her. Words
flowed from her pen to be published in 1843, and
again under the dateline of February 21, 1844.
In fact, whole paragraphs from her pen found
their way into *Rambles*.

The cave passed through a succession of own-
ers from 1798 until the spring of 1838 when it
was owned by the brothers Hyman and Simon

Gratz, merchants of Philadelphia. During most of
the intervening years it was managed by resident
agents, the most recent in 1837 being Robinson
Shackelford and Archibald Miller, Jr.

Although the cave was famous, lack of decent
access roads discouraged all but the most
hardy and most determined visitors. Stagecoaches
stopped nine miles from the entrance, at Bell's
Tavern. The remaining distance was over rugged
country along the single road that led to the cave.
Rough and uneven in dry weather, it was almost
impassable during wet seasons. The last lap of the
journey was often finished on horseback.

There was an inn of sorts at the cave. It was a
log building with two rooms on the ground floor,
each 18 feet square, with a 10-foot open space
between, and an upper story over all. But most of
the overnight visitors, at least those who had the
money, preferred to sleep and eat at Bell's.

Any enterprising businessman could envision
that with passable roads to the cave and accept-
able accommodations on the grounds, a flourishing business could be developed in showing the
cave. Such was the plan of Franklin Gorin (1798–
1877), an attorney of Glasgow, Kentucky, in the
adjoining county. On April 17, 1838, he and A. A.
Harvey signed papers to purchase the cave from
the Gratz brothers for the sum of $5000, to be
paid in annual installments of $1000 on the first
day of each year for five years.

Gorin retained Archibald Miller, Jr. as resident

manager and began improvements at the cave.
The inn was enlarged to sleep 30 to 40 persons;
fences and stables were built; and a new cave
guide was added. The guide was Gorin's slave, a
17-year old lad named Stephen. Manager Miller
and Joseph Shackelford, sons of former tenant
guides, taught young Stephen the routes and
passages in the cave, just as they had been taught
by their fathers. Thus began the unique career of
Stephen L. Bishop (1821–1857), a slave who became a legend in his own lifetime.

During the summer of 1838, Stephen familiar-
ized himself with every room, every corridor, and
every passageway known to previous guides. More
than that, he began to blaze new trails in the darkness where others had never gone before. Some
of these were through confusing mazes, up and
down as well as horizontal. Beyond one such maze
was a tremendous vertical void, the largest dome-
pit yet found. Mammoth Cave had yielded another of its secrets. Gorin gave it his name, and
Gorin's Dome (pp. 61–63) was added to the
itinerary of sights shown the paying public.

Newspaper descriptions of this new discovery
brought adventurers eager to join in further explorations. One of the cave passages led to a deep
pit. The passage continued beyond the pit, but the
pit was so wide and deep that explorers during the
previous 40 years had not been able to cross it.
With their feeble lights they could not even see
the bottom, so they called it the Bottomless Pit,

a name taken from the Bible.

October 20, 1838, was a red-letter day in the history of Mammoth Cave. H. C. Stephenson, a visitor from Georgetown, Kentucky, and guide Stephen stood at the brink of Bottomless Pit. Cautiously they placed a ladder across the pit and gingerly crossed over to the other side (pp. 64–65). The cave went on, and on. And so did they, as far as the oil for their lamps permitted. Then they retraced their steps to the entrance and up the hill to the inn. Triumphantly, they announced their discovery to the others.

No time was lost in spanning the pit with a wooden bridge. Guides and visitors alike used the bridge for further explorations. Within days they had explored Pensico Avenue (pp. 66–70), Bunyan's Way (p. 66), the Winding Way (p. 71), Relief Hall (p. 72), and River Hall (p. 79), and had reached the River Styx (p. 81) at the lowest level in the cave.

Reports of these discoveries brought an increased number of visitors, and more guides were needed to accommodate them. In 1839 Gorin hired two slaves of Thomas Bransford of Nashville, Tennessee, for the annual sum of $100 each. The new guides were the brothers Materson (Mat) and Nicholas (Nick). Stephen taught them the cave, and they shared in discoveries yet to come.

These activities did not escape the notice of Dr. John Croghan (1790–1849), an enterprising

Louisville physician and Kentucky businessman (p. 53). On October 8, 1839, he purchased the cave for $10,000. Many new improvements were soon to be made.

Croghan was the son of Major William Croghan (1752–1822), a veteran of the Revolution, and Lucy Clark Croghan (1765–1838). His mother was the sister of General George Rogers Clark (1752–1818). John's brother, Colonel George Croghan (1791–1849), was the Inspector General of the United States Army, and his brother-in-law, General Thomas S. Jesup (1788–1860), was Quartermaster General of the United States Army.

The future owner of Mammoth Cave was reared at the Croghan family home known as Locust Grove, just east of Louisville. He attended Priestley's Seminary in Danville, Kentucky, and graduated from the College of William and Mary in Williamsburg, Virginia. Thereafter he studied medicine under the celebrated Dr. Benjamin Rush (1745–1813) in Philadelphia and received a Doctor of Medicine degree at the University of Pennsylvania in 1813.

After graduation Croghan returned to Louisville aboard the steamboat *Comet*. He opened an office for the practice of medicine in Louisville and entered into the social and cultural life of the city. He took an active part in the establishment of the Louisville Marine Hospital, on land now occupied by the Louisville General Hospital, and served as one of its directors from 1817 until 1832.

Croghan took an increasing interest in commercial matters, at first related to medicine, and later in other fields. Upon the death of his father at Locust Grove in 1822, John inherited over 5000 acres of land in central Kentucky south of Green River, where his father had been a deputy surveyor. At least as early as 1824, Croghan had conducted business matters with Franklin Gorin, who remained his business agent for a number of years thereafter. In 1825 John's brother, Nicholas, took a trip through Mammoth Cave. In large bold letters high on the right wall of Gothic Avenue near Booth's amphitheatre, he inscribed his name: Ns. Croghan, May 7, 1825.

For three years beginning in 1826, Dr. Croghan engaged in the business of producing salt on an 800-acre tract that he owned south of Columbia, Kentucky. This was the home of Dr. Nathan Gaither (1788–1862), one of the south-central Kentucky physicians who believed that Mammoth Cave could be used to treat certain diseases, especially respiratory disorders. Gaither had suggested that the Commonwealth of Kentucky purchase Mammoth Cave and establish a hospital in one of its corridors. More than likely, Croghan and Gaither discussed this novel use of the cave, for such was mentioned by the author of *Rambles* (p. 46). In 1829, Dr. Croghan leased his salt works, and Dr. Gaither began his first term as Representative in Congress.

Croghan sailed for Europe in 1832, where he learned that Englishmen had as much knowledge of Mammoth Cave as many Americans. Returning in 1833 to Locust Grove, he found that his services as a medical practitioner were as much in demand as before. However, he spent more and more time administering his farming interests. In fact, he rather enjoyed his role as a gentleman farmer.

In 1838, Dr. Robert M. Bird's classic description of Mammoth Cave was republished in the second volume of *Peter Pilgrim: or a Rambler's Recollections*. This was enough to stir the boy in any man's heart. Moreover, Dr. Bird reported that the saltpetre miners who had entered the cave in poor health were soon restored to perfect health while working there (p. 47). Would a stay in the cave of a few weeks or months, mused Croghan, actually cure respiratory disorders? Would it cure consumption?

For years medical men had searched for a way to cure this disease. Occasionally a doctor would make public announcement that he had discovered a treatment and cure for pulmonary consumption, but such claims proved false when their patients continued to languish and die. Dr. Bird had directed the attention of medical men to Mammoth Cave and the curative properties of the cave atmosphere. They speculated that perhaps the nitrates in the cave air, or its uniform temperature, or a combination of these and perhaps unknown factors had a therapeutic effect.

Also in 1838, the new discoveries made in the cave greatly increased its size and its popularity. During the winter of 1838–1839 this was a frequent topic of conversation among the knowledgeable citizenry of Louisville, and Croghan was one of the most knowledgeable. He was a long-time business acquaintance of Franklin Gorin, who had recently purchased the cave. Gorin had already made sizeable expenditures to improve the property, and another $1000 installment on the purchase price was due the following January.

Opportunity knocked on Croghan's door, and he welcomed it. As a businessman he knew that better roads and a good hotel would make the cave a profitable commercial enterprise. As a physician he envisioned a center for the treatment of invalids within the cave. Dr. John Croghan bought Mammoth Cave.

A good hotel was the first priority. Adding to the existing structure, Croghan hired Joseph C. Shackelford to build two log buildings, each with four rooms, a 12-foot hall, and a second story. To these were added 16 cottages. Later a larger two-story building 30 x 90 feet was constructed. The first floor of this building was the dining room, the second the ballroom. All of these buildings were connected and constituted the Mammoth Cave Hotel, which must have been an excellent one indeed by the standards of that time (pp. vii and 11).

At his own expense, Dr. Croghan began building roads to the cave. A public road was opened from Cave City to the Mammoth Cave Hotel; this road continued from the hotel across Green River to connect with a road to Grayson Springs. Another road began at the Louisville and Nashville Turnpike near Rowletts Station and led to the hotel, then on southwest near Dripping Spring, where it connected again with the turnpike (p. vi). This was reported to be a splendid road across rough country. Not only was this the shortest route between Louisville and Nashville, but more to the point, it passed immediately in front of the Mammoth Cave Hotel (bypassing Bell's Tavern). The new hotel became a stage stop for the colorful four-horse stages. Travelers stopped at the hotel for the night, visited the cave the next day, often staying three or four days to see the cave, and thereby paying more money for hotel accommodations and meals than for cave trips. Croghan had demonstrated again that he was a good businessman.

Archibald Miller, Jr. (pp. 11 and 24) was retained as manager. Stephen, Mat, and Nick continued as guides; Alfred was added to the guide staff. Cave trips were formulated ranging from two miles to nine miles to suit the convenience of the hotel guests. Those who came especially to see the cave could stay an entire week at the hotel and see different parts of the cave each day they took an underground excursion.

Even as the new roads and hotel were being
built. Croghan received inquiries from physicians
who wished to send their patients to the cave for
treatment. Cottages were built within the cave to
house them. The first patient to arrive was Dr.
William J. Mitchell of Glasgow, Kentucky, himself a physician, who had diagnosed his own ail-
ment as pulmonary consumption. In the summer
of 1842 he took up residence in the cave. At the
end of five weeks he pronounced himself "very
much relieved" and left.

This apparent success was welcome news to
other doctors and their patients. Additional cottages were built, and patients came from New
York, Pennsylvania, South Carolina, Alabama,
and Kentucky. Those with terminal illnesses died
in the cave. The experiment failed. By the spring
of 1843 all of the cottages were empty. Another
episode in the varied history of Mammoth Cave
had ended (p. 46).

But the exploration of the never-ending passages continued. Adventuresome visitors and the
guides continued to make new discoveries. During
1839 they went beyond the River Styx (p. 81) to
the Lethe (p. 82) and beyond that to Echo River
(p. 83).

In November, 1840, Stephen and a visitor with
a zest for exploration climbed the right wall of
River Hall (pp. 72 and 79), passed Bandit's Hall
(p. 73), and followed a long muddy stoopway.
At its end they found another dome-pit. This was

even larger than Gorin's Dome. Another major discovery had been made. The following month, a
larger party returned with ropes. Led by Stephen
and Mat, they entered the pit and found new
cave passages which surpassed all their expecta-
tions. None of them had ever seen anything like
it before. It was mammoth, and Mammoth Dome
(pp. 74–78) became another cave sight to thrill
and awe the visitors who followed.

Echo River was crossed in 1840 and cave
explorers entered the many branching passages
beyond (p. 85). Stephen's reputation as the principal cave guide increased with each new discovery. He was fearless and dependable. Visitors
who entered the cave for exploration insisted that
he be assigned as their guide. In July, 1841, John
Craig of Philadelphia, Brice Patton of Louisville,
and Stephen (p. 91) were in a cave corridor far
beyond the rivers. Working their way up into a
higher cross passage, they discovered a new avenue containing many strange and beautiful gypsum formations on the walls and ceilings.

In one area, the ceiling was covered with white
gypsum nodules that looked like snowballs thrown
against it (p. 93). At other places the gypsum was
more delicate and fragile, like the bloom of flowers, glistening, sparkling, beautiful in the illumination of their cave lights. Stephen had shared
in another noteworthy discovery.

Specimens of the stone cave flowers were sent
to Professor Locke, who wrote that alabaster had

been found in Mammoth Cave. All learned men
knew of Professor Parker Cleaveland at Bowdoin
College in Brunswick, Maine. His extensive collection of mineral crystals together with the cabinet in which they were displayed had become
world famous. Scientific men often referred to
"Cleaveland's Cabinet of Crystals," and the laity
used the term "Cleaveland's Cabinet" to denote
any large display of beautiful and unusual stone
crystals. The new avenue decorated so profusely
with gypsum crystals was another Cleaveland's
Cabinet, and it was so named (pp. 90–99).

Beyond this new avenue, the guide Mat discov-
ered a charming little room which Dr. Croghan
named Serena's Arbor (p. 96) for his niece,
Serena Croghan, the daughter of Colonel George
Croghan. Likewise Croghan named Angelica's
Grotto (p. 70) in Pensaco Avenue for her sister,
Angelica Croghan. The stone dining table (p. 98)
in Cleaveland's Avenue was named for Angelica's
sister-in-law, Cornelia. The area of the stone
grapes east of the Snowball room was named
Mary's Vineyard in honor of another niece, Mary
Jesup, the daughter of General Thomas S. Jesup.

The dramatic discoveries made since the crossing of Bottomless Pit outdated the Mammoth
Cave books written by Lee in 1835 and Dr. Bird
in 1838. Cave visitors in 1840 needed a new guidebook. Some of them sought employment from Dr.
Croghan to write it for him, but he had another
author in mind. On January 18, 1841, he wrote

Victor Audubon, the son of his old friend John J. Audubon (1785–1851):

I have been applied to by several artists to allow them to take views of the Cave, to write descriptions thereof and to publish the same in a quarto volume. If I thought you would undertake it, I would allow the privilege of doing so to no one but yourself.

Audubon did not accept the invitation, and Croghan resumed his search for a suitable author. Knowing that illustrations would enhance the book, he procured from an artist by the name of Campbell a number of views to be used in the book. A letter dated July 26, 1842, written from Mammoth Cave to Ebenezer Meriam (1794–1864) at Brooklyn, New York, states:

Mr. Allen and Mr. Campbell, artists of great merit, have been for some time engaged in taking views of the Cave. The painting of Stalagmite Hall, the Church, the great Domes, the Bandit's Hall, the river scenery, &c., will be peculiarly interesting. The work, which will be a large one, containing descriptions of the cave generally, and particularly of the scenes represented, will be written by some competent writer, and it, as well as the engravings, will be published in England or Scotland.

Just as the previous books about the cave were woefully out of date, so were the previous maps — and for the same reason. At least five different maps of Mammoth Cave had been made between

1810 and 1835, three of which had been published. All of them stopped at Bottomless Pit. By
the fall of 1841 the greater part of the cave, and
its most interesting features, lay beyond the pit.

While John Croghan was still looking for a
"competent writer," his brother George procured
a new and up-to-date map of the cave in a matter
of days. During the winter of 1841–1842 (when
there was little if any business at the cave) Dr.
Croghan brought Stephen back home with him
to Locust Grove. Col. George Croghan was also
there, and on January 6, 1842, he wrote in his
journal that he

> had Stephen busily employed drawing in pen-
> cil a map of the cave.

Twelve days later, on Tuesday, January, 18th, he
wrote:

> engaged from supper til bed time in drawing or
> rather inking a pencil drawing of the cave by
> Stephen the guide.

Three years later Stephen's map was published
by Dr. Croghan in *Rambles*. In the meantime,
copies of the map were made for use at the cave.
Stephen was given full credit for drafting the new
map, and his reputation continued to grow, not
only at the cave where he reigned as sovereign
guide but also nationally in 1843 and 1844 in an
increasing number of publications about the cave.

One of the cave visitors in 1844 was Alexander
Clark Bullitt (1807–1868), the son of Thomas

and Diana Moore Bullitt. Like the Croghans, the Bullitts were socially prominent in Louisville. John Croghan had been romantically interested in Alex's sister, Mary, during the middle 1820's, and later in her younger sister, Eloise. Bullitt had worked for the *Louisville Journal* and later was the editor of the *New Orleans Picayune*. During the years, John and Alex had become old friends: John an eminent Louisville physician and the owner of Mammoth Cave, Alex a professional journalist.

Croghan's written language as disclosed by his extensive correspondence is formal, serious, and stilted. By contrast, journalists write with imagination, use descriptive adjectives generously, and breathe life into their narratives. Croghan's search for a suitable author ended when Alex Bullitt visited the cave in 1844, perhaps as Croghan's guest.

Besides Bullitt's personal observations, he could and did draw upon a wealth of materials already written about the cave. His final text of *Rambles in the Mammoth Cave during the year 1844* included excerpts from at least six prior publications. Ebenezer Meriam is quoted verbatim on pages 20, 21, 25–33, 75–78, 90, and 91. Passages from Edmund F. Lee's *Notes on the Mammoth Cave* appear on pages 51–52, 55–57, and 86–87. The published words of Dr. Robert Montgomery Bird are repeated on pages 14–17, 21, 33–36, 47–48, and 101. Whole paragraphs by Lydia Maria Child are reprinted on pages 79–82, 85, 89, and 90.

References are made to the findings of Dr. John Locke at pages 50, 86, and 90. A sixth source is reported on page 91 to be the *New York Christian Observer* (the original of which has eluded an extensive search), quoted on pages 91–97.

Either Dr. Croghan or his brother George is believed to have written the *Publisher's Advertisement* on pages v–vii, signed by the initial "C."

John Croghan was the publisher in the sense that he paid the cost of having the book printed and took charge of its distribution, sales at the cave, and gifts to his friends and acquaintances, especially those who might visit the cave and spend a week or so at his new hotel. With this in mind, he had inserted on page x the *Table of Distances* from various cities and towns to Mammoth Cave, and also the *Interesting Facts* on pages viii–ix. Significantly missing from these *Facts* is any reference to the length of the cave, a point of controversy from 1810 until the 1970's. Instead, the *Interesting Facts* stresses the safety and the freedom from supposed annoyances of parties visiting the cave.

In December 1844, Croghan invited the Louisville firm of Morton & Griswold to submit a bid for printing the book. They replied on December 18, 1844 as follows:

We will print one thousand copies of your book on Mammoth Cave, not to exceed 120 pages of the 12to size for twenty-three cents per copy. Paper to be of handsome quality and to be bound in neat half morocco with cloth sides, lettered and filletted on the back. If the book when printed should exceed the above specified number of pages, the additional charge to be only in proportion.

If you request it, we will advance the requisite sums for such engravings as you may determine on, the sums so advanced to be added to the 23 cents per copy as above specified, to be repaid us on settlement.

The completed book consisted of 101 pages and included six engravings of the views made by Campbell and the map by Stephen Bishop. The author was not named. Instead, the title page merely listed the author as "A Visiter." Perhaps, Bullitt had no objection to remaining anonymous, especially since so many other authors had contributed unwittingly to the book. But it was generally known during the following years that Alex Bullitt was the author. One copy of the *Rambles* book that I examined has a handwritten notation on the title page immediately following the words "By A Visiter" which reads as follows:

Alex Bullitt from facts furnished by Stephen Bishop Guide.

Other handwritten notes throughout the book indicate that they may have been made during the year 1851. On the title page of another copy of *Rambles* that I examined, the following is written in longhand following the words "By A Visiter":

Alex Bullitt, from notes furnished by Stephen,
the guide. So Mr. Alex Griswold, son of Publisher Griswold, informs me. The same information is found on the title page of his (A.G.'s)
copy, which was owned by his father.

R. Ellsworth Call

Richard Ellsworth Call (1856–1917), M.D., Ph.D.,
was a Mammoth Cave enthusiast during the
1890's and the author of several works pertaining
to the cave. His statement that the personal copy
of *Rambles* belonging to Mr. Griswold (who
printed the book) also had the same information
on its title page is impressive evidence that Bullitt
was the author.

Rev. Horace Carter Hovey (1833–1914), whose
book *Celebrated American Caverns* was first published in 1882, referred to *Rambles* and stated that
it was "supposed to be by Alexander Bullett, Esq."
(Hovey 1882, p. 61). Rev. Hovey was religiously
careful in verifying information before using it,
and Dr. Call was meticulously accurate in writing
about Mammoth Cave.

Why, then, have the large libraries fortunate
enough to have a copy of *Rambles* among their
rare books attributed its authorship in recent years
to John Croghan? The answer is only now emerging. These libraries obtained catalog cards with
information pertaining to authors from the Library
of Congress. The Library of Congress first cata-
loged *Rambles* in 1916 and tentatively designated

John Croghan as its author. This was done using the best sources of information then available, but certainly not sources based on information known by Rev. Hovey and Dr. Call. Nor could the Library have considered the factual data set out in the foregoing pages, most of which was located only within the last 20 years, and some of which is published herein for the first time.

The sources of information used by the Library of Congress in 1916 relied on the facts that John Croghan was the owner of Mammoth Cave when the book was published and that the *Publisher's Advertisement* was followed by his initial "C." The inferences assumed the dignity of authority. Dutifully, librarians neatly penciled Croghan's name on the title page of their copies. Thus, the 20th century substituted his name for the anonymous author of *Rambles.*

But Dr. Croghan did not publish the book in 1845 to confuse the librarians of the next century. His principal interest was to increase the popularity of the cave, and *Rambles* served his purposes admirably. It portrayed the cave as easily accessible, accommodations comfortable, and cave trips safe and pleasurable for ladies as well as gentlemen. It gave Mammoth Cave a new look. More and more affluent Louisville families came to the cave hotel as a summer resort during the hot summer weeks. More and more cultured travelers considered it as necessary to visit Mammoth Cave as Niagara Falls. *Rambles* became a reference book to remind visitors of the sights they had seen, and a source book for authors who were to write other books about the cave.

Rambles also added to the popularity and to the legend of Stephen Bishop. His map in the book reminded its readers that, although a slave on the surface, he was monarch in the cave. Sought after by scientists, authors, and celebrities as their guide, he conducted them along the underground avenues with dignity and confidence. The most reserved and genteel persons trusted their safety to his care. Journalists praised his manners and his knowledge of the cave. After he died in 1857, his legend lived on. More than 20 years later a visitor from Pennsylvania arranged for a tombstone to be placed at his grave on the hill south of the cave entrance. The grave marker incorrectly gave the date of his death as 1859, and this date remains as a part of the legends and traditions of Mammoth Cave.

Dr. John Croghan died on January 11, 1849, at Locust Grove, reportedly from "an affected liver and a kind of pulmonary consumption." It is ironic that he fell victim to consumption, a disease he had sought to treat in the cave. He never married. By his will, he devised Mammoth Cave to his nephews and nieces in trust and made detailed testamentary provisions for its future management. During the ten years Croghan owned the cave, he developed it into a major tourist attraction; from his grave he controlled its destinies for the next three-quarters of a century.

Books had been written about Mammoth Cave before, but after the appearance of *Rambles* the flood gates opened, and Mammoth Cave literature flowed from the presses. Four bibliographies have been published; the latest, by the Potamological Institute of the University of Louisville (1962), contains 768 references. Obscured by this avalanche of publications, *Rambles* was all but forgotten. And yet, in the opinion of cave historians, it is one of the all-time classics of Mammoth Cave literature.

Harold Meloy
Shelbyville, Indiana

Acknowledgments

Samuel W. Thomas, Louisville historian, supplied most of the biographical material on the life and works of John Croghan. Others who assisted in the gathering of materials used herein are: Eugene H. Conner, Ruth Atwood, and Joan Titley, also of the University of Louisville; Garner B. Hanson, of Park City, Kentucky; Ellis Jones, of Cave City, Kentucky; Evelyn R. Dale, Curator, the Filson Club, Louisville, Kentucky; Riley Handy, Reference Librarian, Kentucky Library, Bowling Green, Kentucky; John F. Bridge, Roger

W. Brucker, Stanley D. Sides, Gordon L. Smith,
and Patty Jo Watson, of the Cave Research Foun-
dation; William R. Halliday, editor of the *Journal
of Spelean History*; and William V. Westphal,
Mary Giesecke, Cecil Ray France, Lewis Cutliff,
Parker Ritter, Edmond Logsdon, Albert C. Coats,
Fred Furlong, and Arthur Furlong, of the National
Park Service at Mammoth Cave.

BIBLIOGRAPHY

Blane, William N. *An Excursion Through the United States and Canada.* London: Baldwin, Cradock & Joy, 1824.

Bird, Robert Montgomery. *Peter Pilgrim: or a Rambler's Recollections.* Volume 2. Philadelphia: Lea & Blanchard, 1838.

Child, Lydia Marie. "Mammoth Cave," *National Anti-Slavery Standard* (New York), No. 28 (November 30, 1843), p. 104.

Child, Lydia Marie. *Letters from New York, Second Series.* New York: C. S. Francis & Co., 1845. Letter VIII dated February 21, 1844, pp. 75–95.

Conner, Eugene H. "Chronica Medica Kentuckiensis," *Bulletin of the Jefferson County Medical Society* (Louisville), 13, No. 4, May 1965, pp. 17, 40–41.

Conner, Eugene H., M.D. and Samuel W. Thomas, Ph.D. 1966. "John Croghan (1790–1849): An Enterprising Kentucky Physician," *The Filson Club History Quarterly* (Louisville), 40, No. 3, (July 1966), pp. 205–234.

Croghan, John. Letters, reports, records, and legal instruments (*mss.*) *in* the Violet Blair Collection, Henry E. Huntington Library, San Marino, California.

Croghan, John. Letters and records (*mss.*) in the Thomas S. Jesup Papers, Library of Congress.

Faust, Burton. *Saltpetre Mining in Mammoth Cave, Ky.* Louisville: The Filson Club. 1967.

Holmes, Issac. "Mammoth Cave in Kentucky" *in: An Account of the United States of America,* pp. 439–454. London: Caxton Press, 1823.

Hovey, Horace Carter. *Celebrated American Caverns.* Cincinnati: Robert Clarke & Co., 1882. Reprinted with a New Introduction by William R. Halliday, New York: Johnson Reprint Corporation, 1970.

Lee, Edmund F. *Notes on the Mammoth Cave.* Cincinnati: James and Gazley, 1835.

Meloy, Harold. "Early Maps of Mammoth Cave," *Journal of Spelean History* (Seattle, Washington), 1, No. 3, 1968, pp. 49–57. 1968.

Meloy, Harold. "The Gatewoods at Mammoth Cave," *Journal of Spelean History* (Seattle, Washington), 2, No. 3, 1969, pp. 51–62. 1969.

Meloy, Harold. *Mummies of Mammoth Cave.* Shelbyville, Indiana: Micron, 1971.

Meriam, Ebenezer. "Mammoth Cave," *New York Municipal Gazette,* 1, No. 17 (February 21, 1844), pp. 317–324.

Sides, Stanley D. and Harold Meloy. "The Pursuit of Health in the Mammoth Cave," *Bulletin of the History of Medicine* (Baltimore: Johns Hopkins Press), 45, No. 4, 1971, pp. 367–379.

Thomas, Samuel W., Eugene H. Conner, and Harold Meloy. 1970. "A History of Mammoth Cave, Emphasizing Tourist Development and Medical Experimentation under Dr. John Croghan," *The Register of the Kentucky Historical Society*

(Frankfort, Kentucky), 68, No. 4, 1970, pp. 319–340.

Thompson, Ralph Seymour. *The Sucker's Visit to the Mammoth Cave*. Springfield, Ohio: Live Patron Publishing Office, 1879. Rpt. with a New Introduction by John F. Bridge, New York: Johnson Reprint Corporation, 1970.

Vigne, Godfrey T. *Six Months in America*. Vol. 2. London: Whittaker, Treacher and Co., 1832.

Ward, Nahum. *The Wonderful Mammoth Cave in Kentucky*. Liverpool, England: E. Smith and Co., 1817. A broadside. In broadside collection in the Kentucky Library, Western Kentucky University, Bowling Green, Kentucky.

Wilkes, Frank G. *Bibliography of Mammoth Cave National Park*. Louisville, Kentucky: Potamological Institute, University of Louisville, 1962.

MAMMOTH CAVE.

ERRATA.

Page 11th, fifth line from the bottom; for *faltering*, read pattering.

" 46th, eighth line from the top —"They are well furnished, and, without question, *would with* good and comfortable accommodations, pure air, and uniform temperature, cure the pulmonary consumption. *The* invalids in the Cave ought to be cured, &c.,"

read,

They are well furnished, and, without question, *if* good and comfortable accommodations, pure air, and uniform temperature, *could* cure the pulmonary consumption, *the* invalids in the Cave ought to be cured.

Page 101, last line : read. "It has no brother: it *is like* no brother"

RAMBLES

IN THE

MAMMOTH CAVE,

DURING THE YEAR 1844,

BY A VISITER.

LOUISVILLE, KY.:
MORTON & GRISWOLD.
1845.

Printed by MORTON & GRISWOLD.

PUBLISHER'S ADVERTISEMENT.

To meet the calls so frequently made upon us by intelligent visiters to our City, for some work descriptive of the Mammoth Cave, we are, at length, enabled to present the public a succinct, but instructive narrative of a visit to this "Wonder of Wonders," from the pen of a gentleman, who, without professing to have explored ALL that is curious or beautiful or sublime in its vast recesses, has yet seen every thing that has been seen by others, and has described enough to quicken and enlighten the curiosity of those who have never visited it.

Aware of the embarrassment which most persons experience who design visiting the Cave, owing to the absence of any printed itinerary of the various routes leading to it, we have supplied, in the present volume, this desideratum, from information received from reliable persons residing on the different roads here enumerated. The road from Louisville to the Cave, and thence to Nashville, is graded the entire distance, and the greater part of it M'Adamized. From Louisville to the mouth of Salt river, twenty miles, the country is level, with a rich alluvial soil, probably at some former period the bed of a lake. A few miles below the former place and extending to the latter, a chain of elevated hills is seen to the South-East, affording beautiful and picturesque situations for country seats, and strangely overlooked by the rich and tasteful. The river is crossed by a ferry, and the traveler is put down at a comfortable inn in the village of West Point. Two miles from the mouth of Salt river, begins the ascent of Muldrow's Hill. The road is excellent, and having elevated hills on either side, is highly romantic to its summit, five miles. From the top of this hill to Elizabethtown, the country is well settled, though the improvements are generally indifferent—the soil thin, but well adapted to small-grain, and oak the prevailing growth. Elizabethtown, twenty-five miles from the mouth of Salt river, is quite a pretty and flourishing village, built chiefly of brick, with several churches and three large inns. From this place to Nolin creek, the distance is ten miles. Here there is a small town, containing some ten or twelve log houses, a large saw and grist mill, and a comfortable and very neat inn, kept by Mr. Mosher. Immediately after crossing this creek, the traveler enters "Yankee Street," as the inhabitants style this section of the road. For a distance of ten or twelve miles from Nolin toward Bacon creek, the land belongs, or did belong to the former Postmaster General, Gideon Granger, and on either side of the road, to the extent of Mr. G.'s possessions, are settlements made by emigrants from New York and the New England States. From Bacon creek to Munfordsville, eight miles, the country is pleasantly undulating, and here, indeed the whole route from Elizabethtown to the Cave, passes through what was until recently a Prairie, or, in the language of the country, "Barrens," and renders it highly interesting, especially to the botanist, from the multitude and variety of flowers with which it abounds during the Spring and Autumn months. Munfordsville, and Woodsonville directly opposite, are situated on Green river, on high and broken ground. They are small places, in each of which, however, are comfortable inns. Boats laden with tobacco and other produce, descend from this point and from a considerable distance above, to New Orleans. About two and a half miles beyond Mumfordsville, the new State road to the Cave, (virtually made by Dr. Croghan, at a great expense,) leaves the Turnpike, and joins it again at the Dripping Springs, eight miles below, on the route to Nashville. This road, in going from Louisville to Nashville, is not only the shortest by three and a half miles, but to the Cave it is from ten to twelve miles shorter than the one taken by visiters previous to its construction. It therefore lessens the inconvenience, delay and consequent expense to which travelers were formerly subjected. The road itself is an excellent one, the country through which it passes highly picturesque, and Dr. Croghan has entitled himself to the gratitude of the traveling community by his liberality and enterprise in constructing it.

Persons visiting the Cave by Steamer, (a boat leaves Louisville for Bowling-Green every week) will find much to interest them in the admirable locks and dams, rendering the navigation of Green river safe and good at all seasons for boats of a large class. Passengers can obtain conveyances at all times and at moderate rates, from Bowling-Green, by the Dripping Spring, to the Cave, distant twenty-two miles. Fifteen miles of this road is M'Adamized, the remainder is graded and not inferior to the finished portion. The last eight miles from the Dripping Spring to the

Cave, cannot fail to excite the admiration of every one who delights in beholding wild and beautiful scenery. A visit to the Cedar Springs on this
route, is alone worth a journey of many miles. Passengers on the upper
turnpike, from Bardstown to Nashville, can, on reaching Glasgow, at all
times procure conveyances to the Cave, either by Bell's or by Prewett's
Knob.

Arrived at the Cave, the visitor alights at a spacious hotel, the general
arrangements, attendance and *cuisine* of which, are adapted to the most
fastidious taste. He feels that as far as the "creature comforts" are necessary to enjoyment, the prospect is full of promise; nor will he be disap-
pointed. And now, this first and most important preliminary to a traveler
settled to his perfect content, he may remain for weeks and experience
daily gratification, "*Stephen* his guide," in wandering through some of its
two hundred and twenty-six avenues—in gazing, until he is oppressed
with the feeling of their magnificence, at some of its forty-seven domes,—
in listening, until their drowsy murmurs pain the sense, to some of its many water-falls,—or haply intent upon discovery, he hails some new vista,
or fretted roof, or secret river, or unsounded lake, or crystal fountain, with
as much rapture as Balboa, from " that peak in Darien," gazed on the Pa-
cific; he is assured that he "has a poet," and an historian too. Stephen has
linked his name to dome, or avenue, or river, and it is already immortal
—in the Cave.

Independent of the attractions to be found in the Cave, there is much
above ground to gratify the different tastes of visiters. There is a capacious ball-room, ninety feet by thirty, with a fine band of music,—a ten-pin
alley,—romantic walks and carriage-drives in all directions, rendered easy
of access by the fine road recently finished. The many rare and beautiful
flowers in the immediate vicinity of the Cave, invite to exercise, and bou-
quets as exquisite as were ever culled in garden or green-house, may be
obtained even as late as August. The fine sport the neighborhood affords
to the hunter and the angler—Green river, just at hand, offers such "store
of fish," as father Walton or his son and disciple Cotton, were they alive
again, would love to meditate and angle in!—and the woods! Capt. Scott
or Christopher North himself, might grow weary of the sight of game,
winged or quadruped.   C.

INTERESTING FACTS.

1. ACCIDENTS of no kind have ever occurred in the Mammoth Cave.

2. Visiters, going in or coming out of the Cave, are not liable to contract colds; on the contrary, colds are commonly relieved by a visit in the Cave.

3. No impure air exists in any part of the Cave.

4. Reptiles, of no description, have ever been seen in the Cave; on the contrary, they, as well as quadrupeds, avoid it.

5. Combustion is perfect in all parts of the Cave.

6. Decomposition and consequent putrefaction are unobservable in all parts of the Cave.

7. The water of the Cave is of the purest kind; and, besides fresh water, there are one or two sulphur springs.

8. There are two hundred and twenty-six Avenues in the Cave; forty-seven Domes; eight Cataracts, and twenty-three Pits.

9. The temperature of the Cave is 59° Fahrenheit, and remains so, uniformly, winter and summer.

10. No sound, not even the loudest peal of thunder, is heard one quarter of a mile in the Cave.

THE author of "Rambles in the Mammoth Cave," has written a scientific account of the Cave, embracing its Geology, Mineralogy, etc., which we could not, in time, insert in this publication.

TABLE OF DISTANCES.

FROM LOUISVILLE TO MAMMOTH CAVE.

Medley's	10 miles.
Mouth Salt River	10
Trueman's	8
Haycraft's	7
Elizabethtown	9
Nolin	9
Lucas	11
Munfordsville	10
Mammoth Cave	14½

88½ miles

FROM LEXINGTON TO MAMMOTH CAVE.

Harrodsburgh	20 miles.
Perryville	10
Frosts	12
Young	4
Lebanon	7
New Market	12
Barbee	6
Somerville	3
Carters	5
Moss	5
Mitchell	12
Curls	7
Greens	10
Dickeys	8
Mammoth Cave	9

130 miles

FROM GLASGOW TO MAMMOTH CAVE, via.

Dickeys	18 miles.

FROM NASHVILLE TO MAMMOTH CAVE.

Gees	9 miles.
Tyree Springs	13
Buntons	12
Franklin	10
Bowling Green	20
Pattersons	12
Dripping Springs	3
Mammoth Cave	8

87 miles.

FROM BARDSTOWN TO MAMMOTH CAVE.

New Haven	15 miles.
McDougals	10
McAchran (Cobb's stand)	12
Bear Wallow	20
Dickeys (Prewett's Knob)	7
Mammoth Cave	9

73 miles.

FROM BARDSTOWN TO MAMMOTH CAVE, via. MUNFORDSVILLE.

McAchran (Cobb's stand)	37 miles.
Munfordsville	12
Mammoth Cave	14½

63½ miles

FROM GLASGOW TO MAMMOTH CAVE, via.

Bells	18 miles.

CONTENTS.

MAMMOTH CAVE.

CHAPTER I.

THE MAMMOTH CAVE is situated in the County of Edmondson and State of Kentucky, equidistant from the cities of Louisville and Nashville, (about ninety miles from each,) and immediately upon the nearest road between those
two places. Green River is within half a mile
of the Cave, and since the improvements in its
navigation, by the construction of locks and
dams, steam-boats can, at all seasons, ascend to
Bowling Green, distant but twenty-two miles,

and, for the greater part of the year, to the Cave itself.

In going to the Cave from Munfordsville, you will observe a lofty range of barren highlands to the North, which approaches nearer and nearer the Cave as you advance, until it reaches to within a mile of it. This range of highlands or cliffs, composed of calcareous rock, pursuing its rectilinear course, is seen the greater part of the way as you proceed on towards Bowling Green; and, at last, looses itself in the counties below. Under this extensive range of cliffs it is conjectured that the great subterranean territory mainly extends itself.

For a distance of two miles from the Cave, as you approach it from the South-East, the country is level. It was, until recently, a prairie, on which, however, the oak, chestnut and hickory are now growing; and having no underbrush, its smooth, verdant openings present, here and there, no unapt resemblance to the parks of the English nobility.

Emerging from these beautiful woodlands, you suddenly have a view of the hotel and adjacent grounds, which is truly lovely and picturesque.

The hotel is a large edifice, two hundred feet long by forty-five wide, with piazzas, sixteen feet wide, extending the whole length of the building, both above and below, well furnished, and kept in a style, by Mr. Miller, that cannot fail to please the most fastidious epicure.

The Cave is about two-hundred yards from the hotel, and you proceed to it down a lovely and romantic dell, rendered umbrageous by a forest of trees and grape vines; and passing by the ruins of saltpetre furnaces and large mounds of ashes, you turn abruptly to the right and behold the mouth of the great cavern and as suddenly feel the coldness of its air.

It is an appalling spectacle,—how dark, how dismal, how dreary. Descending some thirty feet down rather rude steps of stone, you are fairly under the arch of this "nether world"— before you, in looking outwards, is seen a small stream of water falling from the face of the crowning rock, with a wild faltering sound, upon the ruins below, and disappearing in a deep pit, —behind you, all is gloom and darkness!

Let us now follow the guide—who, placing on his back a canteen of oil, lights the lamps,

and giving one to each person, we commence
our subterranean journey; having determined to
confine ourselves, for this day, to an examination of *some* of the avenues on this side of the
rivers, and to resume, on a future occasion, our
visit to the fairy scenes beyond. I emphasize
the word *some* of the avenues, because no visiter
has ever yet seen one in twenty; and, although
I shall attempt to describe only a few of them,
and in so doing will endeavor to represent things
as I saw them, and as they impressed me, I am
not the less apprehensive that my descriptions
will appear as unbounded exaggerations, so wonderfully vast is the Cave, so singular its formations, and so unique its characteristics.

At the place where our lamps were lighted,
are to be seen the wooden pipes which conducted the water, as it fell from the ceiling, to the
vats or saltpetre hoppers; and near this spot too,
are interred the bones of a *giant*, of such vast
size is the skeleton, at least of such portions of
it as remain. With regard to this giant, or
more properly skeleton, it may be well to state,
that it was found by the saltpetre workers far
within the Cave years ago, and was buried by

their employer where it now lies, to quiet their superstitious fears, not however before it was bereft of its head by some fearless antiquary.

Proceeding onward about one-hundred feet, we reached a door, set in a rough stone wall, stretched across and completely blocking up the Cave; which was no sooner opened, than our lamps were extinguished by the violence of the wind rushing outwards. An accurate estimate of the external temperature, may at any time, be made, by noting the force of the wind as it blows inward or outward. When it is very warm without, the wind blows outwards with violence; but when cold, it blows inwards with proportionate force. The temperature of the Cave, (winter and summer,) is invariably the same—59° Fahrenheit; and its atmosphere is perfectly uniform, dry, and of most extraordinary salubrity.

Our lamps being relighted, we soon reached a narrow passage faced on the left side by a wall, built by the miners to confine the loose stone thrown up in the course of their operations, when gradually descending a short distance, we

5*

entered the great vestibule or ante-chamber of
the Cave. "What do we now see? Midnight!
—the blackness of darkness!—Nothing! Where
is the wall we were lately elbowing out of the
way? It has vanished!—It is lost! We are
walled in by darkness, and darkness canopies us
above. Look again;—Swing your torches aloft!
Aye, now you can see it; far up, a hundred feet
above your head, a grey ceiling rolling dimly
away like a cloud, and heavy buttresses, bending
under the weight, curling and toppling over their
base, begin to project their enormous masses
from the shadowy wall. How vast! How solemn! How awful! The little bells of the brain
are ringing in your ears; you hear nothing else
—not even a sigh of air—not even the echo of
a drop of water falling from the roof. The
guide triumphs in your look of amazement and
awe; he falls to work on certain old wooden
ruins, to you, yet invisible, and builds a brace or
two of fires, by the aid of which you begin to
have a better conception of the scene around
you. You are in the vestibule or ante-chamber,
to which the spacious entrance of the Cave, and

the narrow passage that succeeds it, should be
considered the mere gate-way and covered approach.   It is a basilica of an oval figure—two-
hundred feet in length by one-hundred and fifty
wide, with a roof which is as flat and level as
if finished by the trowel of the plasterer, of fifty
or sixty or even more feet in height.   Two
passages, each a hundred feet in width, open
into it at its opposite extremities, but at right
angles to each other; and as they preserve a
straight course for five or six-hundred feet, with
the same flat roof common to each, the appearance to the eye, is that of a vast hall in the
shape of the letter L expanded at the angle, both
branches being five-hundred feet long by one-
hundred wide.   The passage to the right hand
is the " Great Bat Room;" (Audubon Avenue.)
That in the front, the beginning of the Grand
Gallery, or the Main Cavern itself.   The whole
of this prodigious space is covered by a single
rock, in which the eye can detect no break or
interruption, save at its borders, where is a broad,
sweeping cornice, traced in horizontal panel-
work, exceedingly noble and regular; and not a
single pier or pillar of any kind contributes to

support it.   It needs no support.   It is like the arched and ponderous roof of the poet's mausoleum :

"By its own weight made stedfast and immoveable."

The floor is very irregularly broken, consisting of vast heaps of the nitrous earth, and of the ruins of the hoppers or vats, composed of heavy planking, in which the miners were accustomed to leach it.   The hall was, in fact, one of their chief factory rooms.   Before their day, it was a cemetery ; and here they disinterred many a mouldering skeleton, belonging it seems, to that gigantic eight or nine feet race of men of past days, whose jaw-bones so many vivacious persons have clapped over their own, like horse-collars, without laying by a single one to convince the soul of scepticism.

Such is the vestibule of the Mammoth Cave, —a hall which hundreds of visitors have passed through without being conscious sf its existence. The path, leading into the Grand Gallery, hugs the wall on the left hand ; and is, besides, in a hollow, flanked on the right hand by lofty mounds of earth, which the visitor, if he looks at

them at all, which he will scarcely do, at so
early a period after entering, will readily suppose
to be the opposite walls. Those who enter the
Great Bat Room, (Audubon Avenue,) into
which flying visitors are seldom conducted, will
indeed have some faint suspicion, for a moment,
that they are passing through infinite space; but
the walls of the Cave being so dark as to reflect
not one single ray of light from the dim torches,
and a greater number of them being necessary to
disperse the gloom than are usually employed,
they will still remain in ignorance of the grandeur around them."

Such is the vestibule of the Mammoth Cave,
as described by the ingenious author of "Calavar," "Peter Pilgrim," &c.

From the vestibule we entered Audubon Avenue, which is more than a mile long, fifty or sixty
feet wide and as many high. The roof or ceiling exhibits, as you walk along, the appearance
of floating clouds—and such is observable in
many other parts of the Cave. Near the termination of this avenue, a natural well, twenty-five
feet deep, and containing the purest water, has
been recently discovered; it is surrounded by

stalagmite columns, extending from the floor to
the roof, upon the incrustations of which, when
lights are suspended, the reflection from the
water below and the various objects above and
around, gives to the whole scene an appearance
equally rare and picturesque. This spot, however, being difficult of access, is but seldom visited.

The Little Bat Room Cave—a branch of
Audubon Avenue,—is on the left as you advance, and not more than three-hundred yards
from the great vestibule. It is but little more
than a quarter of a mile in length, and is remarkable for its pit of two-hundred and eighty feet in
depth; and as being the hibernal resort of bats.
Tens of thousands of them are seen hanging
from the walls, in apparently a torpid state, during
the winter, but no sooner does the spring open,
than they disappear.

Returning from the Little Bat Room and Audubon Avenue, we pass again through the vestibule, and enter the Main Cave or Grand Gallery.
This is a vast tunnel extending for miles, avera-
ging throughout, fifty feet in width by as many
in height. It is truly a noble subterranean ave-

nue; the largest of which man has any knowledge, and replete with interest, from its varied
characteristics and majestic grandeur.

Proceeding down the main Cave about a
quarter of a mile, we came to the Kentucky
Cliffs, so called from the fancied resemblance to
the cliffs on the Kentucky River, and descending gradually about twenty feet entered the
church, when our guide was discovered in the
pulpit fifteen feet above us, having reached there
by a gallery which leads from the cliffs. The
ceiling here is sixty three feet high, and the
church itself, including the recess, cannot be
less than one hundred feet in diameter. Eight
or ten feet above and immediately behind the pulpit, is the organ loft, which is sufficiently capacious for an organ and choir of the largest size.
There would appear to be something like design in all this;—here is a church large enough
to accomodate thousands, a solid projection of
the wall of the Cave to serve as a pulpit, and
a few feet back a place for an organ and choir.
In this great temple of nature, religious service
has been frequently held, and it requires but a
slight effort on the part of a speaker, to make himself distinctly heard by the largest congregation.

Sometimes the guides climb up the high and ragged sides, and suspend lamps in the crevices and on the projections of the rock, thus lighting up a scene of wild grandeur and sublimity.

Concerts too have been held here, and the melody of song has been heard, such as would delight the ear of a Catalini or a Malibran.

Leaving the church you will observe, on ascending, a large embankment of lixiviated earth thrown out by the miners more than thirty years ago, the print of wagon wheels and the tracks of oxen, as distinctly defined as though they were made but yesterday; and continuing on for a short distance, you arrive at the Second Hoppers. Here are seen the ruins of the old nitre works, leaching vats, pump frames and two lines of wooden pipes; one to lead fresh water from the dripping spring to the vats filled with the nitrous earth, and the other to convey the lye drawn from the large reservoir, back to the furnace at the mouth of the Cave.

The quantity of nitrous earth contained in the Cave is "sufficient to supply the whole population of the globe with saltpetre."

"The dirt gives from three to five pounds of nitrate of lime to the bushel, requiring a large proportion of fixed alkali to produce the required crystalization, and when left in the Cave become re-impregnated in three years. When saltpetre bore a high price, immense quantities were manufactured at the Mammoth Cave, but the return of peace brought the saltpetre from the East Indies in competition with the American, and drove that of the produce of our country entirely from the market. An idea may be formed of the extent of the manufacture of saltpetre at this Cave, from the fact that the contract for the supply of the fixed alkali alone for the Cave, for the year 1814, was twenty thousand dollars."

" The price of the article was so high, and the profits of the manufacturer so great, as to set half the western world gadding after nitre caves— the gold mines of the day. Cave hunting in fact became a kind of mania, beginning with speculators, and ending with hair brained young men, who dared for the love of adventure the risk which others ran for profit." Every hole, remarked an old miner, the size of a man's body, has been penetrated for miles around the Mammoth Cave, but although we found "*petre earth*," we never could find a cave worth having.

2

CHAPTER II.

In looking from the ruins of the nitre works, to
the left and some thirty feet above, you will see a
large cave, connected with which is a narrow gallery sweeping across the Main Cave and losing
itself in a cave, which is seen above to your right.
This latter cave is the Gothic Avenue, which no
doubt was at one time connected with the cave
opposite and on the same level, forming a com-
plete bridge over the main avenue, but afterwards
broken down and separated by some great con-
vulsion.

The cave on the left, which is filled with sand,
has been penetrated but a short distance; still
from its great size at its entrance, it is more than
probable, that, were all obstructions removed, it
might be found to extend for miles.

On Stone by T. Campbell

Bauer & Tachenacher Lith.

ENTRANCE TO THE GOTHIC AVENUE.

While examining the old saltpetre works, the guide left us without our being aware of it, but casting our eyes around we perceived him standing some forty feet above, on the projection of a huge rock, or tower, which commands a view of the grand gallery to a great extent both up and down.

Leaving the Main Cave and ascending a flight of stairs twenty or thirty feet, we entered the Gothic Avenue, so named from the Gothic appearance of some of its compartments. This avenue is about forty feet wide, fifteen feet high and two miles long. The ceiling looks in many places as smooth and white as though it had been under the trowel of the most skilful plasterer. A good road has been made throughout this cave, and such is the temperature and purity of its atmosphere, that every visitor must experience their salutary influences.

In a recess on the left hand elevated a few feet above the floor and about fifty feet from the head of the stairs leading up from the Main Avenue, two mummies long since taken away, were to be seen in 1813. They were in good preservation; one was a female with her extensive

wardrobe placed before her. The removal of
those mummies from the place in which they
were found can be viewed as little less than
sacrilege. There they had been, perhaps for
centuries, and there they ought to have been left.
What has become of them I know not. One of
them, it is said, was lost in the burning of the
Cincinnati museum. The wardrobe of the female was given to a Mr. Ward, of Massachusetts,
who I believe presented it to the British Museum.

Two of the miners found a mummy in Audubon Avenue, in 1814. With a view to con-
ceal it for a time, they placed large stones over
it, and marked the walls about the spot so that
they might find it at some future period; this
however, they were never able to effect. In
1840, the present hotel keeper Mr. Miller, learn-
ing the above facts, went in search of the place
designated, taking with him very many lights,
and found the marks on the walls, and near to
them the mummy. It was, however, so much
injured and broken to pieces by the heavy
weights which had been placed upon it, as to be
of little interest or value. I have no doubt, that

if proper efforts were made, mummies and other objects of curiosity might be found, which would tend to throw light on the early history of the first inhabitants of this continent.

Believing, that whatever may relate to these mummies cannot fail to interest, I will extract from the recently published narrative of a highly scientific gentleman of New York, himself one of the early visitors to the Cave.

"On my first visit to the Mammoth Cave in 1813, I saw a relic of ancient times, which requires a minute description. This description is from a memorandum made in the Cave at the time.

In the digging of saltpetre earth, in the short cave, a flat rock was met with by the workmen, a little below the surface of the earth in the Cave; this stone was raised, and was about four feet wide and as many long; beneath it was a square excavation about three feet deep and as many in length and width. In this small nether subterranean chamber, sat in solemn silence one of the human species, a female with her wardrobe and ornaments placed at her side. The body was in a state of perfect preservation, and sitting

2*

erect. The arms were folded up and the hands were laid across the bosom; around the two wrists was wound a small cord, designed probably, to keep them in the posture in which they were first placed; around the body and next thereto, was wrapped two deer-skins. These skins appear to have been dressed in some mode different from what is now practised by any people, of whom I have any knowledge. The hair of the skins was cut off very near the surface. The skins were ornamented with the imprints of vines and leaves, which were sketched with a substance perfectly white. Outside of these two skins was a large square sheet, which was either wove or knit. This fabric was the inner bark of a tree, which I judge from appearances to be that of the linn tree. In its texture and appearance, it resembled the South Sea Island cloth or matting; this sheet enveloped the whole body and the head. The hair on the head was cut off within an eighth of an inch of the skin, except near the neck, where it was an inch long. The color of the hair was a dark red; the teeth were white and perfect. I discovered no blemish upon the body, except a wound between two

ribs near the back-bone; one of the eyes had
also been injured. The finger and toe nails
were perfect and quite long. The features were
regular. I measured the length of one of the
bones of the arm with a string, from the elbow
to the wrist joint, and they equalled my own in
length, viz: ten and a half inches. From the
examination of the whole frame, I judged the
figure to be that of a very tall female, say five
feet ten inches in height. The body, at the
time it was first discovered, weighed but fourteen pounds, and was perfectly dry; on expo-
sure to the atmosphere, it gained in weight by
absorbing dampness four pounds. Many persons have expressed surprise that a human body
of great size should weigh so little, as many human skeletons of nothing but bone, exceed this
weight. Recently some experiments have been
made in Paris, which have demonstrated the
fact of the human body being reduced to ten
pounds, by being exposed to a heated atmosphere for a long period of time. The color of
the skin was dark, not black; the flesh was
hard and dry upon the bones. At the side of
the body lay a pair of moccasins, a knapsack

and an indispensable or reticule.   I will describe
these in the order in which I have named them.
The moccasins were made of wove or knit bark,
like the wrapper I have described.   Around the
top there was a border to add strength and perhaps as an ornament.   These were of middling
size, denoting feet of small size.   The shape of
the moccasins differs but little from the deer-skin
moccasins worn by the Northern Indians.   The
knapsack was of wove or knit bark, with a
deep, strong border around the top, and was
about the size of knapsacks used by soldiers.
The workmanship of it was neat, and such as
would do credit as a fabric, to a manufacturer
of the present day.   The reticule was also made
of knit or wove bark.   The shape was much
like a horseman's valise, opening its whole length
on the top.   On the side of the opening and a
few inches from it, were two rows of hoops,
one row on each side.   Two cords were fastened to one end of the reticule at the top, which
passed through the loop on one side and then
on the other side, the whole length, by which
it was laced up and secured.   The edges of the
top of the reticule were strengthened with deep

fancy borders. The articles contained in the knapsack and reticule were quite numerous, and are as follows: one head cap, made of wove or knit bark, without any border, and of the shape of the plainest night cap; seven head-dresses made of the quills of large birds, and put together somewhat in the same way that feather fans are made, except that the pipes of the quills are not drawn to a point, but are spread out in straight lines with the top. This was done by perforating the pipe of the quill in two places and running two cords through these holes, and then winding around the quills and the cord, fine thread, to fasten each quill in the place designed for it. These cords extended some length beyond the quills on each side, so that on placing the feathers erect on the head, the cords could be tied together at the back of the head. This would enable the wearer to present a beautiful display of feathers standing erect and extending a distance above the head, and entirely surrounding it. These were most splendid head dresses, and would be a magnificent ornament to the head of a female at the present day,—several hundred strings of beads; these consisted of a very hard brown seed smaller than hemp seed, in each of which a small hole had been made, and through this hole a small three corded thread, similar in appearance and texture to seine twine; these were tied up in bunches, as a merchant ties up coral beads when he exposes them for sale. The red hoofs of fawns, on a string supposed to be worn around the neck as a necklace. These hoofs were about twenty in number, and may have been emblematic of Innocence; the claw of an eagle, with a hole made in it, through which a cord was passed, so that it could be worn pendent from the neck; the jaw of a bear designed to be worn in the same manner as the eagle's claw, and supplied with a cord to suspend it around the neck; two rattlesnake-skins, one of these had fourteen rattles upon it, these were neatly folded up; some vegetable colors done up in leaves; a small bunch of deer sinews, resembling cat-gut in appearance; several bunches of thread and twine, two and three threaded, some of which were nearly white; seven needles, some of these were of horn and some of bone, they were smooth and appeared to have been much used. These needles had each a knob or whirl on the top, and at the other end were brought to a point like a large sail needle. They had no eyelets to receive a thread. The top of one of these needles was handsomely scalloped; a hand-piece made of deer-skin, with a hole through it for the thumb, and designed probably to protect the hand in the use of the needle, the same as thimbles are now used; two whistles about eight inches long made of cane, with a joint about one third the length; over the joint is an opening extending to each side of the tube of the whistle, these openings were about three-fourths of an inch long and a quarter of an inch wide, and had each a flat reed placed in the opening. These whistles were tied together with a cord wound around them.

I have been thus minute in describing the mute witness from the days of other times, and the articles which were deposited within her earthen house. Of the race of people to whom she belonged when living, we know nothing; and as to conjecture, the reader who gathers from these pages this account, can judge of the matter as well as those who saw the remnant of mortality in the subterranean chambers in which

she was entombed. The cause of the preservation of her body, dress and ornaments is no
mystery. The dry atmosphere of the Cave,
with the nitrate of lime, with which the earth
that covers the bottom of these nether palaces is
so highly impregnated, preserves animal flesh,
and it will neither putrify nor decompose when
confined to its unchanging action. Heat and
moisture are both absent from the Cave, and it is
these two agents, acting together, which produce
both animal and vegetable decomposition and
putrefaction.

In the ornaments, etc., of this mute witness of
ages gone, we have a record of olden time, from
which, in the absence of a written record, we
may draw some conclusions. In the various
articles which constituted her ornaments, there
were no metallic substances. In the make of
her dress, there is no evidence of the use of any
other machinery than the bone and horn needles.
The beads are of a substance, of the use of
which for such purposes, we have no account
among people of whom we have any written
record. She had no warlike arms. By what
process the hair upon her head was cut short,

or by what process the deer-skins were shorn,
we have no means of conjecture. These articles afford us the same means of judging of the
nation to which she belonged, and of their ad-
vances in the arts, that future generations will
have in the exhumation of a tenant of one of
our modern tombs, with the funeral shroud, etc.
in a state of like preservation; with this differ-
ence, that with the present inhabitants of this
section of the globe, but few articles of ornament
are deposited with the body. The features of
this ancient member of the human family much
resembled those of a tall, handsome American
woman. The forehead was high, and the head
well formed."

> " Ye mouldering relics of a race departed,
>   Your names have perished; not a trace remains."

The Gothic Avenue was once called the Haunted Chamber, and owed its name to an adventure that befell one of the miners in former days,
which is thus related by the author of "Calavar."

" In the Lower Branch is a room called the
Salts Room, which produces considerable quantities of the sulphate of magnesia, or of soda,
we forget which — a mineral that the proprietor

of the Cave did not fail to turn to account.　The
miner in question was a new and raw hand — of
course neither very well acquainted with the
Cave itself, nor with the approved modes of
averting or repairing accidents, to which, from
the nature of their occupation, the miners were
greatly exposed.　Having been sent, one day,
in charge of an older workman, to the Salts
Room to dig a few sacks of the salt, and finding
that the path to this sequestered nook was perfectly plain; and that, from the Haunted Chambers being a single, continuous passage without
branches, it was impossible to wander from it,
our hero disdained on his second visit, to seek
or accept assistance, and trudged off to his work
alone.　The circumstance being common enough
he was speedily forgotten by his brother miners;
and it was not until several hours after, when
they all left off their toil for the more agreeable
duty of eating their dinner, that his absence was
remarked, and his heroical resolution to make
his way alone to the Salts Room remembered.
As it was apparent, from the time he had been gone,
that some accident must have happened to him,
half a dozen men, most of them negroes, strip-

ped half naked, their usual working costume, were
sent to hunt him up, a task supposed to be of
no great difficulty, unless he had fallen into a pit.
In the meanwhile, the poor miner, it seems, had
succeeded in reaching the Salts Room, filling
his sack, and retracing his steps half way back
to the Grand Gallery; when finding the distance
greater than he thought it ought to be, the con-
ceit entered his unlucky brain that he *might*
perhaps be going wrong. No sooner had the
suspicion struck him, than he fell into a violent
terror, dropped his sack, ran backwards, then returned, then ran back again — each time more
frightened and bewildered than before; until
at last he ended his adventure by tumbling
over a stone and extinguishing his lamp. Thus
left in the dark, not knowing where to turn,
frightened out of his wits besides, he fell to re-
membering his sins — always remembered by
those who are lost in the Cave — and praying
with all his might for succor. But hours passed away, and assistance came not; the poor
fellow's frenzy increased; he felt himself a doom-
ed man; he thought his terrible situation was a
judgment imposed on him for his wickedness;

nay, he even believed, at last, that he was no
longer an inhabitant of the earth — that he had
been translated, even in the body, to the place
of torment — in other words, that he was in hell
itself, the prey of the devils, who would presently be let loose upon him. It was at this
moment the miners in search of him made their
appearance; they lighted upon his sack, lying
where he had thrown it, and set up a great shout,
which was the first intimation he had of their
approach. He started up, and seeing them in
the distance, the half naked negroes in advance,
all swinging their torches aloft, he, not doubting
they were those identical devils whose appearance he had been expecting, took to his heels,
yelling lustily for mercy; nor did he stop, not-
withstanding the calls of his amazed friends,
until he had fallen a second time over the rocks,
where he lay on his face, roaring for pity,· until,
by dint of much pulling and shaking, he was
convinced that he was still in the world and the
Mammoth Cave." Such is the story of the
Haunted Chambers, the name having been given
to commemorate the incident.

CHAPTER III.

RESUMING our explorations in this most interesting avenue, we soon came in sight of stalagmite pillars, reaching from the floor to the
ceiling, once perhaps white and translucent, but
now black and begrimed with smoke. At this
point we were startled by the hollow tread of
our feet, caused by the proximity of another
large avenue underneath, which the guide assured us he had often visited. In this neighborhood too, there are a number of Stalactites, one of
which was called the Bell, which on being struck,
sounded like the deep bell of a cathedral; but it
now no longer tolls, having been broken in twain
by a visiter from Philadelphia some years ago.
Further on our way, we passed Louisa's Bower
and Vulcan's Furnace, where there is a heap, not

3*

unlike cinders in appearance, and some dark
colored water, in which I suppose the great forger
used to slake his iron and perhaps his bolts.
Next in order and not very distant are the new
and old Register Rooms. Here on the ceiling
which is as smooth and white as if it had been
finished off by the plasterer, thousands of names
have been traced by the smoke of a candle—
names which can create no pleasing associations
or recollections; names unknown to fame, and
which might excite disgust, when read for the
first time on the ceiling which they have dis-
figured.

Soon after leaving the old Register Room,
we were halted by our guide, who took from
us all the lamps excepting one. Having made
certain arrangements, he cried aloud, "Come on!"
which we did, and in a few moments entered
an apartment of surprising grandeur and magnificence. This apartment or hall is elliptical in
shape and eighty feet long by fifty wide. Stalagmite columns, of vast size nearly block up the
two ends; and two rows of pillars of smaller di-
mensions, reaching from floor to ceiling and equidistant from the wall on either side, extend its

On Stone by T. Campbell.

Bauer & Reichemacker's Lith.

STALAGMITE HALL OR GOTHIC CHAPEL.

entire length. Against the pillars, and in many
places from the ceiling, our lamps were hanging,
and, lighting up the whole space, exhibited to
our enraptured sight a scene surpassingly grand,
and well calculated to inspire feelings of solemnity and awe. This is the Stalagmite Hall, or
as some call it, the Gothic Chapel, which no
one can see under such circumstances as did
our party, without being forcibly reminded of
the old, very old cathedrals of Europe. Continuing our walk we came to the Devil's Arm-
Chair. This is a large Stalagmite column, in
the centre of which is formed a capacious seat.
Like most other visiters we seated ourselves in
the chair of his Satanic Majesty, and drank sulphur water dipped up from a small basin of rock,
near the foot of the chair. Further on we passed a number of Stalactites and Stalagmites, Napoleon's Breast-Work, (behind which we found
ashes and burnt cane,) the Elephant's Head, the
Curtain, and arrived at last at the Lover's Leap.
The Lover's Leap is a large pointed rock pro-
jecting over a dark and gloomy hollow, thirty
or more feet deep. Our guide told us that the
young ladies often asked their beaux to take the

Lover's Leap, but that he never knew any to "love hard enough" to attempt it. We descended into the hollow, immediately below the Lover's Leap, and entered to the left and at right-angle with our previous course, a passage or chasm in the rock, three feet wide and fifty feet high, which conducted us to the lower branch of the Gothic Avenue. At the entrance of this lower branch is an immensely large flat rock called Gatewood's Dining Table, to the right of which is a cave, which we penetrated, as far as the Cooling Tub — a beautiful basin of water six feet wide and three deep — into which a small stream of the purest water pours itself from the ceiling and afterwards finds its way into the Flint Pit at no great distance. Returning, we wound around Gatewood's Dining Table, which nearly blocks up the way, and continued our walk along the lower branch more than half a mile, passing Napoleon's Dome, the Cinder Banks, the Crystal Pool, the Salts Cave, etc., etc. Descending a few feet and leaving the cave which continues onwards, we entered, on our right, a place of great seclusion and grandeur, called Annetti's Dome. Through a crevice in the right wall of the dome is a waterfall. The water issues in a stream a foot in diameter, from a high cave in the side of the dome — falls upon the solid bottom, and passes off by a small channel into the Cistern, which is directly on the pathway of the cave. The Cistern is a large pit, which is usually kept nearly full of water.

Near the end of this branch, (the lower branch,) there is a crevice in the ceiling over the last spring, through which the sound of water may be heard falling in a cave or open space above.

Highly gratified with what we had now seen in the Gothic Avenue, we concluded to pursue it no further, but to retrace our steps to the Main Cave, regretting however, that we had not visited the Salts Cave, (a branch of the Gothic Avenue,) on being told, when too late, that it would have amply compensated us for our trouble, being rich in fine specimens of Epsom or Glauber salts.

CHAPTER IV.

WE are now again in the Main Cave or Grand
Gallery, which continues to increase in interest
as we advance, eliciting from our party frequent
and loud exclamations of admiration and wonder.
Not many steps from the stairs leading down
from the Gothic Avenue into the Main Cave,
is the Ball-Room, so called from its singular
adaptedness to such a purpose; for there is an
orchestra, fifteen or eighteen feet high, large
enough to accommodate a hundred or more
musicians, with a gallery extending back to the
level of the high embankment near the Gothic
Avenue; besides which, the avenue here is lofty,
wide, straight and perfectly level for several
hundred feet. At the trifling expense of a plank
floor, seats and lamps, a ball-room might be

had, if not more splendid, at all events more
grand and magnificent than any other on earth.
The effect of music here would be truly inspir-
ing; but the awful solemnity of the place may, in
the opinion of many, prevent its being used as
a temple of Terpsichore. Extremes, we are
told, often meet. The same objection has been
urged against the Cave's being used for religious
services. "No clergyman," "remarked a distinguished divine, "be he ever so eloquent could
concentrate the attention of his congregation in
such a place. The God of nature speaks too
loud here for *man to be heard.*"

Leaving these points to be settled as they
may, we will proceed onwards; the road now is
broad and fine, and in many places dusty. Next
in order is Willie's Spring, a beautifully fluted
niche in the left hand wall, caused by the con-
tinual attrition of water trickling down into a
basin below. This spring derives its name from
that of a young gentleman, the son of a highly re-
spectable clergyman of Cincinnati, who, in the
spirit of romance, assumed the name of Wandering Willie, and taking with him his violin,
marched on foot to the Cave. Wishing no

better place in which to pass the night, he select-
ed this spot, requesting the guide to call for him
in the morning.   This he did and found him
fast asleep upon his bed of earth, with his violin
beside him — ever since it has been called Willie's
Spring.   Just beyond the spring and near the
left wall, is the place where the oxen were fed
during the time of the miners; and strewn around
are a great many corn-cobs, to all appearance,
and in fact, perfectly sound, although they have
lain there for more than thirty years.   In this
neighborhood is a niche of great size in the wall
on the left, and reaching from the roof to the bottom of a pit more than thirty feet deep, down the
sides of which, water of the purest kind is contin-
ually dripping, and is afterwards conducted to a
large trough, from which the invalids obtain their
supply of water, during their sojourn in the Cave.
Near the bottom, this pit or well expands into a
large room, out of which, there is no opening.   It
is probable that Richardson's Spring in the Deserted Chambers is supplied from this well.   Passing
the Well Cave, Rocky Cave, etc., etc., we arrived
at the Giant's Coffin, a huge rock on the right,
thus named from its singular resemblance in

shape to a coffin; its locality, apart from its great size, renders it particularly conspicuous, as all must pass around it, in leaving the Main Cave, to visit the rivers and the thousand wonders beyond. At this point commence those incrustations, which, portraying every imaginable figure on the ceiling, afford full scope to the fanciful to picture what they will, whether of "birds, or beasts, or creeping things." About a hundred yards beyond the Coffin, the Cave makes a majestic curve, and sweeping round the Great Bend or Acute-Angle, resumes its general course. Here the guide ignited a Bengal light. This vast amphitheatre became illuminated, and a scene of enchantment was exposed to our view. Poets may conceive, but no language can describe, the splendor and sublimity of the scene. The rapturous exclamations of our party might have been heard from afar, both up and down this place of wonders. Opposite to the Great Bend, is the entrance of the Sick Room Cave, so called from the fact of the sudden sickness of a visiter a few years ago, supposed to have been caused by his smoking, with others, cigars in one of its most remote and con-

4

fined nooks. Immediately beyond the Great
Bend, a row of cabins, built for consumptive
patients, commences. All of these are framed
buildings, with the exception of two, which are
of stone. They stand in line, from thirty to
one hundred feet apart, exhibiting a picturesque,
yet at the same time, a gloomy and mournful
appearance. They are well furnished, and without question, would with good and comfortable
accommodations, pure air and uniform tempèr-
ature, cure the pulmonary consumption. The
invalids in the Cave ought to be cured; but I
doubt whether the Cave air or any thing else
can cure confirmed Phthisis. A knowledge of
the curative properties of the Cave air, is not,
as is generally supposed, of recent date. It has
been long known. A physician of great respect-
ability, formerly a member of Congress from the
district adjoining the Cave, was so firmly convinced of the medical properties of its air, as to
express more than twenty years ago, as his opinion, that the State of Kentucky ought to purchase it, with a view to establish a hospital in
one of its avenues. Again the author of "Calavar," himself a distinguished professor of med-

icine, makes the following remarks in relation
to the Cave air, as far back as 1832, the date
of his visit:

"It is always temperate. Its purity, judging
from its effects on the lungs, and from other circumstances, is remarkable, though in what its
purity consists, I know not. But, be its compo-
sition what it may, it is certain its effects upon
the spirits and bodily powers of visiters, are extremely exhilarating; and that it is not less salu-
brious than enlivening. The nitre diggers were
a famously healthy set of men; it was a common and humane practice to employ laborers of
enfeebled constitutions, who were soon restored
to health and strength, though kept at constant
labour; and more joyous, merry fellows were
never seen. The oxen, of which several were
kept day and night in the Cave, hauling the
nitrous earth, were after a month or two of toil,
in as fine condition for the shambles, as if fatten-
ed in the stall. The ordinary visiter, though
rambling a dozen hours or more, over paths of
the roughest and most difficult kind, is seldom
conscious of fatigue, until he returns to the upper
air; and then it seems to him, at least in the

summer season, that he has exchanged the atmosphere of paradise for that of a charnel warm-
ed by steam—all without is so heavy, so dank,
so dead, so mephitic.   Awe and even apprehen-
sion, if that has been felt, soon yield to the in-
fluence of the delicious air of the Cave; and
after a time a certain jocund feeling is found
mingled with the deepest impressions of sublimity, which there are so many objects to awaken.
I recommend all broken hearted lovers and
dyspeptic dandies to carry their complaints to
the Mammoth Cave, where they will undoubt-
edly find themselves "translated" into very bux-
om and happy persons before they are aware
of it."

On Stone by T. Campbell

Bauer & Messieurmacher Lith.

STAR CHAMBER.

CHAPTER V.

THE Star Chamber next attracted our attention. It presents the most perfect optical illu-
sion imaginable; in looking up to the ceiling,
which is here very high, you seem to see the
very firmament itself, studded with stars; and
afar off, a comet with its long, bright tail. Not
far from this Star Chamber, may be seen, in a
cavity in the wall on the right, and about twenty
feet above the floor, an oak pole about ten
feet long and six inches in diameter, with two
round sticks of half the thickness and three feet
long, tied on to it transversely, at about four feet
apart. By means of a ladder we ascended to
the cavity, and found the pole to be firmly fixed
—one end resting on the bottom of the cavity,
and the other reaching across and forced into a

4*

crevice about three feet above. We supposed that this was a ladder once used by the former inhabitants of the Cave, in getting the salts which are incrusted on the walls in many places. Doct. Locke, of the Medical College of Ohio, is, however, of the opinion, that on it was placed a dead body,— similar contrivances being used by some Indian tribes on which to place their dead. Although thousands have passed the spot, still this was never seen until the fall of 1841. Ages have doubtless rolled by since this was placed here, and yet it is perfectly sound ; even the bark which confines the transverse pieces shows no marks of decay.

We passed through some Side Cuts, as they are called. These are caves opening on the sides of the avenues; and after running for some distance, entering them again. Some of them exceed half a mile in length ; but most generally they are short. In many of them, " quartz, calcedony, red ochre, gypsum, and salts are found." The walking, in this part of the avenue, being rough, we progressed but slowly, until we reached the Salts Room ; here we found the walls and ceiling covered with salts hanging in crystals.

The least agitation of the air causing flakes of
the crystals to fall like snow. In the Salts
Room are the Indian houses, under the rocks—
small spaces or rooms completely covered—some
of which contain ashes and cane partly burnt."
The *Cross Rooms*, which we next come to, is
a grand section of this avenue; the ceiling has
an unbroken span of one hundred and seventy
feet, without a column to support it! The
mouths of two caves are seen from this point,
neither of which we visited, and much to our
loss, as will appear from the following extract
from the "Notes on the Mammoth Cave, by E.
F. Lee, Esq., Civil Engineer," in relation to one
of them—the Black Chambers:

"At the ruins in the Black Chambers, there
are a great many large blocks composed of different strata of rocks, cemented together, resembling the walls, pedestals, cornices, etc., of some
old castle, scattered over the bottom of the Cave.
The avenue here is so wide, as to make it quite
a task to walk from one side to the other. On
the right hand, beyond the ruins, you enter the
right branch, on the same level—the ceiling of
which is regularly arched. Through the Big

Chimneys you ascend into an upper room, about the size of the Main Cave, the bottom of which is higher than the ceiling of the one below. Proceeding on we soon heard the low murmurings of a water-fall,—the sound of which becomes louder and louder as we advanced, until we reached the Cataract. In the roof are perforations as large as a hogshead, on the right hand side, from which water is ever falling, on ordinary occasions in not very large quantities; but after heavy rains—in torrents; and with a horrible roar that shakes the walls and resounds afar through the Cave. It is at such times that these cascades are worthy the name of cataracts, which they bear. The water falling into a great funnel-shaped pit, immediately vanishes."

Here we concluded to dine, and at quite a fashionable hour—4, P. M. The guide arranged the plates, knives and forks, wine-glasses, etc., on a huge table of rock, and announced,—"Dinner is ready!" We filled our plates with the excellent viands prepared at the Cave House, and seating ourselves on the rocks or nitre earth, partook of our repast with the gusto of gourmands, and quaffing, ever and anon, wines which would have done credit to the Astor or Tremont House. "There may be," remarked our corpulent friend B., "a great deal of romance in this way of eating—with your plate on your lap, and seated on a rock or a lump of nitre earth— but for my part I would rather dispense with the poetry of the thing and eat a good dinner, whether above or below ground, from off a bona-fide table, and seated in a good substantial chair. The proprietor ought to have at all the "watering places, (and they are numerous,) tables, chairs, and the necessary table furniture, that visitors might partake of their collations in some degree of comfort." The guide who, by the way, is a very intelligent and facetious fellow, was much amused at the suggestion of our friend, and remarked that "the owner of the Cave, Doct. Croghan, lived near Louisville, and that the only way to get such '*fixings*' at the watering places, was to write to him on the subject." "Then," said B., "for the sake of those who may follow after us, I will take it upon myself to write."

From this point you have a view of the Main Avenue on our left, pursuing its general course,

and exhibiting the same solemn grandeur as from
the commencement,—and directly before us the
way to the Humble Chute and the Cataract.
The Humble Chute is the entrance to the Solitary Chambers; before entering which, we must
crawl on our hands and knees some fifteen or
twenty feet under a low arch. It is appropri-
ately named; as is the Solitary Chambers which
we have now entered. You feel here,—to use
an expression of one of our party,—"out of the
world." Without dwelling on the intervening
objects—although they are numerous and not
without interest,—we will enter at once the
Fairy Grotto of the Solitary Cave. It is in truth
a fairy grotto; a countless number of Stalactites
are seen extending, at irregular distances, from
the roof to the floor, of various sizes and of the
most fantastic shapes—some quite straight,
some crooked, some large and hollow—forming
irregularly fluted columns; and some solid near
the ceiling, and divided lower down, into a great
number of small branches like the roots of trees;
exhibiting the appearance of a coral grove.
Hanging our lamps to the incrustations on the
columns, the grove of Stalactites became faintly

lighted up, disclosing a scene of extraordinary
wildness and beauty. " This is nothing to what
you'll see on the other side of the rivers," cries
our guide, smiling at our enthusiastic admiration.
With all its present beauty, this grotto is far
from being what it was, before it was despoiled
and robbed some eight or nine years ago, by a
set of vandals, who, through sheer wantonness,
broke many of the stalactites, leaving them
strewn on the floor—a disgustful memorial of
their vulgar propensities and barbarian-like con-
duct.

Returning from the Fairy Grotto, we entered
the Main Cave at the Cataract, and continued
our walk to the Chief City or Temple, which is
thus described by Lee, in his "Notes on the
Mammoth Cave:"

" The Temple is an immense vault covering
an area of two acres, and covered by a single
dome of solid rock, one hundred and twenty
feet high. It excels in size the Cave of Staffa;
and rivals the celebrated vault in the Grotto of
Antiparos, which is said to be the largest in the
world. In passing through from one end to the
other, the dome appears to follow like the sky

in passing from place to place on the earth. In
the middle of the dome there is a large mound
of rocks rising on one side nearly to the top,
very steep and forming what is called the *Mountain*. When first I ascended this mound from
the cave below, I was struck with a feeling of
awe more deep and intense, than any thing that
I had ever before experienced. I could only
observe the narrow circle which was illuminated
immediately around me; above and beyond
was apparently an unlimited space, in which
the ear could catch not the slightest sound, nor
the eye find an object to rest upon. It was
filled with silence and darkness; and yet I knew
that I was beneath the earth, and that this space,
however large it might be, was actually bounded
by solid walls. My curiosity was rather excited
than gratified. In order that I might see the
whole in one connected view, I built fires in
many places with the pieces of cane which I
found scattered among the rocks. Then taking
my stand on the Mountain, a scene was presented of surprising magnificence. On the opposite
side the strata of gray limestone, breaking up by
steps from the bottom, could scarcely be dis-

On Stone by T. Campbell

CHIEF CITY OR TEMPLE

Danforth Lithographers Lith.

cerned in the distance by the glimmering light.
Above was the lofty dome, closed at the top
by a smooth oval slab, beautifully defined in
the outline, from which the walls sloped away on
the right and left into thick darkness. Every
one has heard of the dome of the Mosque
of St. Sophia, of St. Peter's and St. Paul's;
they are never spoken of but in terms of admiration, as the chief works of architecture,
and among the noblest and most stupendous
examples of what man can do when aided by
science; and yet when compared with the dome
of this Temple, they sink into comparative in-
significance. Such is the surpassing grandeur
of Nature's works."

To us, the Temple seemed to merit the glow-
ing description above given, but what would
Lee think, on being told, that since the discovery
of the rivers and the world of beauties beyond
them, not one person in fifty visits the Temple
or the Fairy Grotto; they are now looked upon
as tame and uninteresting. The hour being now
late, we concluded to proceed no further, but to
return to the hotel, where we arrived at 11, P. M.

5

CHAPTER VI.

On being summoned to breakfast the next morning, we ascertained that a large party of ladies and gentlemen had arrived during our absence, who, like ourselves, were prepared to enter the Cave. They, however, were for hurrying over the rivers, to the distant points beyond—we, for examining leisurely the avenues on this side. At 8 o'clock, both parties accompanied by their respective guides and making a very formidable array, set out from the hotel, happy in the anticipation of the "sights to be seen." It was amusing to hear the remarks, and to witness the horror of some of the party on first beholding the mouth of the Cave. Oh! it is so

frightful!—It is so cold!—I *cannot* go in! Not-
withstanding all this, curiosity prevailed, and
down we went—arranged our lamps, which
being extinguished in passing through the door-
way by the strong current of air rushing outwards, there arose such a clamor, such laughter,
such screaming, such crying out for the guides,
as though all Bedlam had broke loose,—the
guides exerting themselves to quiet apprehensions, and the visiters of yesterday knowing that
there was neither danger nor just cause of alarm,
doing their utmost to counteract their efforts, by
well feigned exclamations of terror. At length the
lamps were re-lighted and order being restored,
onward we went. The Vestibule and Church
were each in turn illuminated, to the enthusiastic
delight of all—even those of the party, who
were but now so terrified, were loud in their
expressions of admiration and wonder. Arrived
at the Giant's Coffin, we leave the Main Cave
to enter regions very dissimilar to those we have
seen. A narrow passage behind the Coffin
leads to a circular room, one hundred feet in diameter, with a low roof, called the Wooden
Bowl, in allusion to its figure, or as some say,

from a wooden bowl having been found here by some old miner. This Bowl is the vestibule of the Deserted Chambers. On the right, are the Steeps of Time, (why so called we are left to conjecture,) down which, descending about twenty feet, and almost perpendicularly for the first ten, we enter the Deserted Chambers, which in their course present features extremely wild, terrific and multiform. For two hundred yards the ceiling as you advance is rough and broken, but further on, it is waving, white and smooth as if worn by water. At Richardson's Spring, the imprint of moccasins and of children's feet, of some by-gone age, were recently seen. There are more pits in the Deserted Chambers than in any other portion of the Cave; and among the most noted are the Covered Pit, the Side-Saddle Pit and the Bottomless Pit. Indeed the whole range of these chambers, is so interrupted by pits, and throughout is so irregular and serpentine and so bewildering from the number of its branches, that the visiter, doubtful of his footing, and uncertain as to his course, is soon made sensible of the prudence of the regulation, which enjoins him, "not to leave the guide." "The

Covered Pit is in a little branch to the left;
this pit is twelve or fifteen feet in diameter,
covered with a thin rock, around which a narrow crevice extends, leaving only a small support on one side.   There is a large rock resting
on the centre of the cover.   The sound of a
waterfall may be heard from the pit but cannot
be seen."   The Side-Saddle Pit is about twenty
feet long and eight feet wide, with a margin
about three feet high, and extending lengthwise
ten feet, against which one may safely lean, and
view the interior of the pit and dome.   After a
short walk from this place, we came to a ladder
on our right, which conducted us down about
fifteen feet into a narrow pass, not more than
five feet wide; this pass is the Labyrinth, one end
of which leads to the Bottomless Pit, entering it
about fifty feet down, and the other after various windings, now up, now down, over a
bridge, and up and down ladders, conducts you
to one of the chief glories of the Cave, — Gorin's
Dome; which, strange to tell, was not discovered until a few years ago.   Immediately behind
the ladder, there is a narrow opening in the
rock, extending up very nearly to the cave above,

5*

which leads about twenty feet back to Louisa's
Dome, a pretty little place of not more than
twelve feet in diameter, but of twice that height.
This dome is directly under the centre of the
cave we had just been traversing, and when
lighted up, persons within it can be plainly seen
from above, through a crevice in the rock.   Arrived at Gorin's Dome, we were forcibly struck
by the seeming appearance of *design*, in the
arrangement of the several parts, for the special
accommodation of visiters — even with reference
to their number.   The Labyrinth, which we
followed up, brought us at its termination, to a
window or hole, about four feet square, three
feet above the floor, opening into the interior
of the dome, about midway between the bottom
and top; the wall of rock being at this spot,
not more than eighteen inches thick; and continuing around, and on the outside of the dome,
along a gallery of a few feet in width, for twenty
or more paces, we arrived at another opening
of much larger size, eligibly disposed, and com-
manding, like the first, a view of very nearly the
whole interior space.   Whilst we are arranging
ourselves, the guide steals away, passes down,

down, one knows not how, and is presently
seen by the dim light of his lamp, fifty feet below,
standing near the wall on the inside of the dome.
The dome is of solid rock, with sides apparently
fluted and polished, and perhaps two hundred
feet high. Immediately in front and about thirty
feet from the window, a huge rock seems suspended from above and arranged in folds like a
curtain. Here we are then, the guide fifty feet
below us. Some of the party thrusting their
heads and, in their anxiety to see, their bodies
through the window into the vast and gloomy
dome of two hundred feet in height. The window is not large enough to afford a view to all
at once, they crowd one on the top of the other;
the more cautious, and those who do not like
to be squeezed, stand back; but still holding fast
to the garments of their friends for fear they
might in the ecstasy of their feelings, leap into the
frightful abyss into which they are looking. Suddenly the guide ignites a *Bengal light*. The
vast dome is radiant with light. Above, as far
as the eye can reach, are seen the shining sides of
the fluted walls; below, the yawning gulf is rendered the more terrific, by the pallid light ex-

posing to view its vast depth, the whole dis-
playing a scene of sublimity and splendor, such
as words have not power to describe.   Returning, we ascended the ladder near Louisa's Dome,
and continued on, having the Labyrinth on our
right side until it terminates in the Bottomless
Pit.   This pit terminates also the range of the
Deserted Chambers, and was considered the Ul-
tima Thule of all explorers, until within the last
few years, when Mr. Stephenson of Georgetown,
Ky. and the intrepid guide, Stephen, conceived
the idea of reaching the opposite side by throwing a ladder across the frightful chasm.   This
they accomplished, and on this ladder, extending across a chasm of twenty feet wide and
near two hundred deep, did these daring explorers cross to the opposite side, and thus open the
way to all those splendid discoveries, which
have added so much to the value and renown of
the Mammoth Cave.   The Bottomless Pit is
somewhat in the shape of a horse-shoe, having
a tongue of land twenty seven feet long, running
out into the middle of it.   From the end of this
point of land, a substantial bridge has been
thrown across to the cave on the opposite side.

On Stone by T. Campbell

BOTTOMLESS PIT.

Lauer & Zschmacher's Lith.

While standing on the bridge, the guide lets down a lighted paper into the deep abyss; it descends twisting and turning, lower and lower, and is soon lost in total darkness, leaving us to conjecture, as to what may be below. Crossing the bridge to the opposite cave, we find ourselves in the midst of rocks of the most gigantic size lying along the edge of the pit and on our left hand. Above the pit is a dome of great size, but which, from its position, few have seen. Proceeding along a narrow passage for some distance, we arrived at the point from which diverge two noted routes—the Winding Way and Pensico Avenue. Here we called a short halt; then wishing our newly formed acquintances a safe voyage over the "deep waters," we parted; they taking the left hand to the Winding Way and the rivers, and we the right to Pensico Avenue.

CHAPTER VII.

PENSICO AVENUE averages about fifty feet in width, with a height of about thirty feet; and is said to be two miles long. It unites in an eminent degree the truly beautiful with the sublime, and is highly interesting throughout its entire extent. For a quarter of a mile from the entrance, the roof is beautifully arched, about twelve feet high and sixty wide, and formerly was encrusted with rosettes and other formations, nearly all of which have been taken away or demolished, leaving this section of the Cave quite denuded. The walking here is excellent; a dozen persons might run abreast for a quarter of a mile to Bunyan's Way, a branch of the avenue, leading on to the river. At this point the avenue changes its features of beauty and

regularity, for those of wild grandeur and sublimity, which it preserves to the end.   The way,
no longer smooth and level, is frequently interrupted and turned aside by huge rocks, which
lie tumbled around, in all imaginable disorder.
The roof now becomes very lofty and imposingly
magnificent; its long, pointed or lancet arches,
forcibly reminding you of the rich and gorgeous
ceilings of the old Gothic Cathedrals, at the
same time solemnly impressing you with the
conviction that this is a "building not made with
hands."   No one, not dead to all the more
refined sensibilities of our nature, but must ex-
claim, in beholding the sublime scenes which
here present themselves, this is not the work of
man! No one can be here without being reminded of the all pervading presence of the great
"Father of all."

"What, but God, pervades, adjusts and agitates the whole!"

Not far from the point at which the avenue
assumes the rugged features, which now char-
acterize it, we separated from our guide, he
continuing his straight-forward course, and we
descending gradually a few feet and entering a

tunnel of fifteen feet wide on our left, the ceiling
twelve or fourteen feet high, perfectly arched
and beautifully covered with white incrustations,
very soon reached the Great Crossings. Here
the guide jumped down some six or eight feet
from the avenue which we had left, into the
tunnel where we were standing, and crossing it,
climbed up into the avenue, which he pursued
for a short distance or until it united with the
tunnel, where he again joined us. In separating
from, then crossing, and again uniting with the
avenue, it describes with it something like the
figure 8. The name, Great Crossings, is not
unapt. It was however, not given, as our
intelligent guide veritably assured us, in honor
of the Great Crossings where the man lives who
killed Tecumseh, but because two great caves
cross here; and moreover said he, "the valiant
Colonel ought to change the name of his place,
as no two places in a State should bear the
same name, and this being the *great* place ought
to have the preference."

Not very far from this point, we ascended a
hill on our left, and walking a short distance
over our shoe-tops in dry nitrous earth, in a

direction somewhat at a right angle with the avenue below, we arrived at the Pine Apple Bush, a large column, composed of a white, soft, crumbling material, with bifurcations extending from the floor to the ceiling. At a short distance, either to the right or left, you have a fine view of the avenue some twenty feet below, both up and down. Why this crumbling stalactite is called the Pine Apple Bush, I cannot divine. It stands however in a charming, secluded spot, inviting to repose ; and we luxuriated in inhaling the all-inspiring air, while reclining on the clean, soft and dry salt petre earth.

All lovers of romantic scenery ought to visit this avenue, and all dyspeptic hypochondriacs and love-sick despondents should do likewise, for there is something wonderfully exhilarating in the air of Pensico. Our friend B. remarked while rolling on the salt petre earth at the Pine Apple Bush, that he felt "especially happy," and whether from sympathy, air or what not, we all partook of the same feeling. The guide seeing the position of our fat friend, and hearing his remark, said, laughing most

6

immoderately, "these sort of feelings would come over one, now and then in the Cave, but wait till you get in the Winding Way and see how you feel then."

Having descended into the avenue we had left, we passed a number of stalactites and stalagmites, bearing a remarkable resemblance to coral, and a hundred or more paces beyond, arrived at a recess on the left, lined with innumerable crystals of dog-tooth spar, shining most brilliantly, called Angelica's Grotto. One would think it almost sacrilege to deface a spot like this; yet, did a Clergyman (the back of the guide being turned,) deliberately demolish a number of beautiful crystals to inscribe the initials of his name.

Returning to the head of Pensico Avenue, we turned to our right, and entered the narrow pass which leads to the river, pursuing which, for a few hundred yards, descending all the while, at one or two places down a ladder or stone steps, we came to a path cut through a high and broad embankment of sand, which very soon conducted us to the much talked of and anxiously looked for Winding Way. The

Winding Way, has, in the opinion of many, been channeled in the rock by the gradual attrition of water. If this be so, and appearances seem to support such belief, at what early age of the world did the work commence? Was it not when "the earth was without form and void," thousands of years perhaps, before the date of the Mosaic account of the Creation? The Winding Way is one hundred and five feet long, eighteen inches wide, and from three to seven feet deep, widening out above, sufficiently to admit the free use of one's arms. It is throughout tortuous, a perfect *zig-zag*, the terror of the Falstaffs and the ladies of "fat, fair and forty," who have an instinctive dread of the trials to come, and are well aware of the merriment that their efforts to *force a passage* will excite among their companions of less length of girdle. Into this winding way, we entered in Indian file, and turning our right side, then our left, twisting this way, then that, had nearly made good the passage, when our *fat friend*, who was puffing and blowing behind us like a high pressure engine, cried out, "Halt, ahead there! I am stuck as tight as a wedge in a log!" Halt we did, when the guide, looking at our friend, who was in truth "wedg'd in the rocky way and sticking fast," cried out, "I told you, when you said at the Pine Apple Bush, that you felt *especially happy*, to wait till you got to the Winding Way, to see how you would feel then!" The imprisoned gentleman soon burst his bonds, not, however, without damage to his indispensables; and at length forcing his way into Relief Hall, he cried out, in the joy of his heart, while stretching himself and wiping the perspiration from his jolly, rubicund face, "never was a name more appropriate given to any place — Relief. I feel already the *expansive faculty* of the atmosphere, I can now breathe again."

Relief Hall, which you enter from the Winding Way, at a right-angle, is very wide and lofty but not long; turning to the right, we reached its termination at River Hall, a distance of per- haps, one hundred yards Here two routes pre- sent themselves; the one to the left conducts to the Dead Sea and the Rivers, and that to the right, to the Bacon Chamber, the Bandit's Hall, the Mammoth Dome and an infinity of other caves, domes, etc. We will speak of the Bacon

Chamber; but before doing so, let us take our lunch. The air or exercise, or probably both, acted as powerful appetizers, and we soon gave proof that we needed not Stoughton's bitters to provoke an appetite. Having discussed a few glasses of excellent Hock, we left the Bacon Chamber, which is a pretty fair representation of a low ceiling, thickly hung with canvassed hams and shoulders; and proceeded to the Bandit's Hall, up a steep ascent of twenty or thirty feet, rendered very difficult, by the huge rocks which obstructed the way and over which we were forced to clamber. The name is indicative of the spot. It is a vast and lofty chamber, the floor covered with a mountainous heap of rocks rising amphitheatrically almost to the ceiling, and so disposed as to furnish at different elevations, galleries or platforms, reaching immediately around the chamber itself or leading off into some of its hidden recesses. The guide is presently seen standing at a fearful height above, and suddenly a Bengal light, blazes up, "when the rugged roof, the frowning cliffs and the whole chaos of rocks are refulgent in the brilliant glare." The sublimity of the scene is beyond the powers of the imagination.

6*

CHAPTER VIII.

Mammoth Dome—First Discoverers—Little Dome—Tale of a Lamp—
Return.

From the Bandit's Hall, diverge two caves; one of which, the left, leads you to a multitude of domes; and the right, to one which, *par excellence*, is called the Mammoth Dome. Taking the right, we arrived, after a rugged walk of nearly a mile, to a platform, which commands an indistinct view of this dome of domes. It was discovered by a German gentleman and the guide Stephen about two years ago, but was not explored until some months after, when it was visited by a party of four or five, accompanied by two guides, and well prepared with ropes, &c. From the platform, the guides were let down about twenty feet, by means of a rope, and upon reaching the ground below, they found themselves on the side of a hill, which, descending about fifty feet, brought them immediately under the Great Dome, from the summit of which, there is a water-fall. This dome is near four hundred feet high, and is justly considered one of the most sublime and wonderful spectacles of this most wonderful of caverns. From the bottom of the dome they ascended the hill to the place to which they had been lowered from the platform, and continuing thence up a very steep hill, more than one hundred feet, they reached its summit. Arrived at the summit, a scene of awful grandeur and magnificence is presented to the view. Looking down the declivity, you see far below to the left, the visiters whom you have left behind, standing on the platform or termination of the avenue along which they had come; and lower down still, the bottom of the Great Dome itself. Above, two hundred and eighty feet, is the ceiling, lost in the obscurity of space and distance. The height of the ceiling was determined by E. F. Lee, civil engineer. This fact in regard to the elevation of the ceiling and the locality of the Great Hall, was subsequently ascertained, by finding on the summit of the hill, (a spot never before trodden by man,) an iron

lamp!! The astonishment of the guides, as
well as of the whole party, on beholding the
lamp, can be easily imagined; and to this day
they would have been ignorant of its history, but
for the accidental circumstance of an old man
being at the Cave Hotel, who, thirty years ago,
was engaged as a miner in the saltpetre establishment of Wilkins & Gratz. He, on being
shown the lamp, said at once, that it had been
found under the crevice pit (a fact that sur-
prised all,); that during the time Wilkins &
Gratz were engaged in the manufacture of saltpetre, a Mr. Gatewood informed Wilkins, that
in all probability, the richest nitre earth was under the crevice pit.   The depth of this pit being
then unknown, Wilkins, to ascertain it, got a
rope of 45 feet long, and fastening this identical
lamp to the end of it, lowered it into the pit, in
the doing of which, the string caught on fire,
and down fell the lamp.   Wilkins made an offer
of two dollars to any one of the miners who
would descend the pit and bring up the lamp.
His offer was accepted by a man, who, in con-
sequence of his diminutive stature, was nick-
named Little Dave; and the rope being made

fast about his waist, he, torch in hand, was lowered to the full extent of the forty-five feet. Being then drawn up, the poor fellow was found
to be so excessively alarmed, that he could scarcely articulate; but having recovered from his fright,
and again with the full power of utterance, he
declared that no money could tempt him to try
again for the lamp; and in excuse for such a
determination, he related the most marvellous
story of what he had seen—far exceeding the
wonderful things which the unexampled Don
Quixote de la Mancha declared he had seen in
the deep cave of Montesinos. Dave was, in
fact, suspended at the height of two hundred
and forty feet above the level below. Such is
the history of the *lamp*, as told by the old miner,
Holton, the correctness of which was very soon
verified; for guides having been sent to the
place where the lamp was found, and persons
at the same time stationed at the mouth of the
crevice pit, their proximity was at once made
manifest by the very audible sound of each
other's voices, and by the fact that sticks thrown
into the pit fell at the feet of the guides below,
and were brought out by them. The distance

from the mouth of the Cave to this pit, falls short
of half a mile; yet to reach the grand apartment
immediately under it, requires a circuit to be
made of at least three miles.   The illumination
of that portion of the Great Dome on the left,
and of the hall on the top of the hill to the right,
as seen from the platform, was unquestionably
one of the most impressive spectacles we had
witnessed; but to be seen to advantage, another
position ought to be taken by the spectator, and
the dome with its towering height, and the hall
on the summit of the hill, with its gigantic stalagmite columns, and ceiling two hundred feet
high, illuminated by the simultaneous ignition of
a number of Bengal lights, judiciously arranged.
Such was the enthusiastic admiration of some
foreigners on witnessing an illumination of the
Great Dome and Hall, that they declared, it alone
would compensate for a voyage across the
Atlantic.   With the partial illumination of the
Great Dome, we closed our explorations on this
side of the rivers, and retracing our steps, reached
the hotel about sun-set.   At mid-night, the party
which separated from us at the entrance of Pensico Avenue, returned from the points beyond
the Echo river.

CHAPTER IX.

Early the next morning, having made all the
necessary preparations for the grand tour, which
we were the more anxious to take from the glow-
ing accounts of the party recently returned, we
entered the cave immediately after an early breakfast, and proceeded rapidly on to River Hall. It
was evident from the appearance of the flood
here, that it had been recently overflown.

"The cave, or the River Hall," remarks a
fair and distinguished authoress, whose description of the river scenery is so graphic, that I
cannot do better than transcribe it throughout:
"The River Hall descends like the slope of a
mountain; the ceiling stretches away—away before you, vast and grand as the firmament at mid-
night." Going on, and gradually ascending and

keeping close to the right hand wall, you observe on your left " a steep precipice, over which you can look down by the aid of blazing missiles, upon a broad black sheet of water, eighty feet below, called the Dead Sea. This is an awfully impressive place ; the sights and sounds of which, do not easily pass from memory. He who has seen it, will have it vividly brought before him, by Alfieri's description of Filippo, ' only a transient word or act gives us a short and dubious glimmer, that reveals to us the abysses of his being—dark, lurid and terrific, as the throat of the infernal pool.' Descending from the eminence, by a ladder of about twenty feet, we find ourselves among piles of gigantic rocks, " and one of the most picturesque sights in the world, is to see a file of men and women passing along those wild and scraggy paths, moving slowly— slowly, that their lamps may have time to illuminate their sky-like ceiling and gigantic walls— disappearing behind high cliffs—sinking into ravines—their lights shining upwards through fissures in the rocks—then suddenly emerging from some abrupt angle, standing in the bright gleam of their lamps, relieved by the towering black

On Stone by T Campbell

RIVER SCENE.

Bauer & Teichmacher's Lith.

masses around them. He, who could paint the
infinite variety of creation, can alone give an
adequate idea of this marvellous region. As you
pass along, you hear the roar of invisible water-
falls; and at the foot of the slope, the river Styx
lies before you, deep and black, overarched with
rock. The first glimpse of it brings to mind,
the descent of Ulysses into hell,

> " Where the dark rock o'erhangs the infernal lake,
> And mingling streams eternal murmurs make."

Across (or rather down) these unearthly waters,
the guide can convey but four passengers at once.
The lamps are fastened to the prow; the im-
ages of which, are reflected in the dismal pool.
If you are impatient of delay, or eager for new
adventures, you can leave your companions lin-
gering about the shore, and cross the Styx
by a dangerous bridge of precipices overhead.
In order to do this, you must ascend a steep cliff,
and enter a cave above, 300 yards long, from an
egress of which, you find yourself on the bank
of the river, eighty feet above its surface, com-
manding a view of those in the boat, and those
waiting on the shore. Seen from this height,

7

the lamps in the canoe glare like fiery eye-balls; and the passengers, sitting there so hushed and motionless, look like shadows. The scene is so strangely funereal and spectral, that it seems as if the Greeks must have witnessed it, before they imagined Charon conveying ghosts to the dim regions of Pluto. Your companions thus seen, do indeed—

> " Skim along the dusky glades,
> Thin airy souls, and visionary shades."

If you turn your eyes from the canoe to the parties of men and women whom you left waiting on the shore, you will see them by the gleam of their lamps, scattered in picturesque groups, looming out in bold relief from the dense darkness around them."

Having passed the Styx, (much the smallest of the rivers,) you walk over a pile of large rocks, and are on the banks of Lethe ; and looking back, you will see a line of men and women descending the high hill from the cave, which runs *over* the river Styx. Here are two boats, and the parties, which have come by the two routes, *down* the Styx or *over* it, uniting, descend the Lethe about a quarter of a mile, the ceiling for the entire distance being very high—certainly not less than fifty feet. On landing, you enter a level and lofty hall, called the Great Walk, which stretches to the banks of the Echo, a distance of three or four hundred yards. The Echo is truly a river: it is wide and deep enough, at all times, to float the largest steamer. At the point of embarkation, the arch is very low, not more than three feet, in an ordinary stage of water, being left for a boat to pass through. Passengers, of course, are obliged to double up, and lie upon each others shoulders, in a most uncomfortable way, but their suffering is of short duration ; in two boat lengths, they emerge to where the vault of the cave is lofty and wide. The boat in which we embarked was sufficiently large to carry twelve persons, and our voyage down the river was one of deep, indeed of most intense interest. The novelty, the grandeur, the magnificence of every thing around elicited unbounded admiration and wonder. All sense of danger, (had any been experienced before,) was lost in the solemn, quiet sublimity of the scene.

The rippling of the water caused by the motion of our boat is heard afar off, beating under the low arches and in the cavities of the rocks. The report of a pistol is as that of the heaviest artillery, and long and afar does the echo resound, like the muttering of distant thunder. The voice of song was raised on this dark, deep water, and the sound was as that of the most powerful choir. A full band of music on this river of echoes would indeed be overpowering. The aquatic excursion was more to our taste than any thing we had seen, and never can the impression it made be obliterated from our memories.

The Echo is three quarters of a mile long. A rise of the water of merely a few feet connects the three rivers. After long and heavy rains, these rivers sometimes rise to a perpendicular height of more than fifty feet; and then they, as well as the cataracts, exhibit a most terrific appearance. The low arch at the entrance of the Echo, can not be passed when there is a rise of water of even two feet. Once or twice parties have been caught on the further side by a sudden rise, and for a time their alarm was great, not knowing that there was an upper cave through which they could pass, that would lead them around the arch to the Great Walk. This upper cave, or passage, is called Purgatory, and is, for a distance of forty feet, so low, that persons have to crawl on their faces, or, as the guides say, *snake it*. We were pleased to learn that this passage would soon be sufficiently enlarged to enable persons to walk through erect. This accomplished, an excursion to Cleveland's Avenue may be made almost entirely by land, at the same time that all apprehensions of being caught beyond Echo will be removed. It is in these rivers, that the extraordinary white eyeless fish are caught—we secured two of them. There is not the slightest indication of an organ similar to an eye, to be discovered. They have been dissected by skillful anatomists, who declare that they are not only without eyes, but also develope other anomalies in their organization, singularly interesting to the naturalist. "The rivers of Mammoth Cave were never crossed till 1840. Great efforts have been made to discover whence they come and whither they go,

7*

yet they still remain as much a mystery as ever
—without beginning or end; like eternity."

> " Darkly thou glidest onward,
>   Thou deep and hidden wave!
> The laughing sunshine hath not look'd
>   Into thy secret cave.
>
> Thy current makes no music—
>   A hollow sound we hear;
> A muffled voice of mystery,
>   And know that thou art near.
>
> No brighter line of verdure
>   Follows thy lonely way
> No fairy moss, or lily's cup,
>   Is freshened by thy play."

According to the barometrical measurement
of Professor Locke, the rivers of the Cave are
nearly on a level with Green River; but the report of Mr. Lee, civil engineer, is widely different. He says, " The bottom of the Little Bat
Room Pit is one hundred and twenty feet *below* the bed of Green River. The Bottomless
Pit is also deeper than the bed of Green River,
and so far as a surveyor's level can be relied on,
the same may be said of the Cavern Pit and
some others." The rivers of the Cave were unknown at the time of Mr. Lee's visit in 1835,
but they are unquestionably *lower* than the bot-

tom of the pits, and receive the water which flows from them. According to the statement of Lee, the bed of these rivers is lower than the bed of Green River at its junction with the Ohio, taking for granted that the report of the State engineers as to the extent of fall between a point above the Cave and the Ohio, be correct, of which there is no doubt. "It becomes, then," continues Mr. Lee, in reference to the waters of the Cave, "an object of interesting inquiry to determine in what way it is disposed of. If it empties into Green River, the Ohio, or the ocean, it must run a great distance under ground, with a very small descent."

CHAPTER X.

HAVING now left the Echo, we have a walk
of four miles to Cleveland's Avenue. The intervening points are of great interest; but it would
occupy too much time to describe them. We
will therefore hurry on through the pass of El
Ghor, Silliman's Avenue, and Wellington's Gallery, to the foot of the ladder which leads up
to the Elysium of Mammoth cave. And here,
for the benefit of the weary and thirsty, and of
all others whom it may interest, coming after
us, be it known, that Carneal's Spring is close
at hand, and equally near, a sulphur spring, the
water of which, equals in quality and quantity
that of the far-famed White Sulphur Spring, of

Virginia. " At the head of the ladder, you find
yourself surrounded by overhanging stalactites,
in the form of rich clusters of grapes, hard as
flint, and round and polished, as if done by a
sculptor's hand. This is called Mary's Vineyard—the commencement of Cleveland's Avenue, the crowning wonder and glory of this subterranean world. Proceeding to the right about,
a hundred feet from this spot, over a rough and
rather difficult way, you reach the base of the
height or hill, on which, stands the Holy Sepulchre. This interesting spot is reached at some
hazard, as the ascent, which is very steep, and
more than twenty feet high, affords no secure
footing, owing to the loose and shingly charac-
ter of the surface, until the height is gained.
Having achieved this, you stand immediately at
the beautiful door-way of the Chapel, or ante-
room of the Sepulchre. This Chapel, which is,
perhaps, twelve feet square, with a low ceiling,
and decorated in the most gorgeous manner, with
well-arranged draperies of stalactite of every
imaginable shape, leads you to the room of
the Holy Sepulchre adjoining, which is without
ornament or decoration of any kind; exhibiting

nothing but dark and bare walls—like a charnel house. In the centre of this room, which stands a few feet below the Chapel, is, to all appearance, a grave, hewn out of the living rock. This is the Holy Sepulchre. A Roman Catholic priest discovered it about three years ago, and with fervent enthusiasm exclaimed, "The Holy Sepulchre!" a name which it has since borne. Returning from the Holy Sepulchre, we commence our wanderings through Cleveland's Avenue—an avenue three miles long, seventy feet wide, and twelve or fifteen feet high—an avenue more rich and gorgeous than any ever revealed to man—an avenue abounding in formations such as are no where else to be seen, and which the most stupid observer could not behold without feelings of wonder and admiration. Some of the formations in the avenue, have been denominated by Professor Locke, oulophilites, or curled leafed stone; and in remarking upon them, he says, "They are unlike any thing yet discovered; equally beautiful for the cabinet of the amateur, and interesting to the geological philosopher." And I, although a wanderer myself in various climes, and somewhat of a mineralogist withal, have never seen or heard of such. Apprehensive that I might, in attempting to describe much that I have seen, color too highly, I will, in lieu thereof, offer the remarks of an intelligent clergyman, extracted from the New York Christian Observer, of a recent date : " The most imaginative poet never conceived or painted a palace of such exquisite beauty and loveliness, as Cleveland's Cabinet, into which you now pass. Were the wealth of princes bestowed on the most skilful lapidaries, with the view of rivaling the splendors of this single chamber, the attempt would be vain. How then can I hope to give you a conception of it? You must see it; and you will then feel that all attempt at description, is futile. The Cabinet was discovered by Mr. Patten, of Louisville, and Mr. Craig, of Philadelphia, accompanied by the guide Stephen, and extends in nearly a direct line about one and a half miles, (the guides say two miles.) It is a perfect arch, of fifty feet span, and of an average height of ten feet in the centre—just high enough to be viewed with ease in all its parts. It is incrusted from end to end with the most beautiful formations, in every variety of form.

The base of the whole, is carbonate (sulphate)
of lime, in part of dazzling whiteness, and perfectly smooth, and in other places crystallized so
as to glitter like diamonds in the light.   Growing from this, in endlessly diversified forms, is a
substance resembling selenite, translucent and
imperfectly laminated.   It is most probably sulphate of lime, (a gypsum,) combined with sulphate of magnesia.   Some of the crystals bear
a striking resemblance to branches of celery, and
all about the same length; while others, a foot
or more in length, have the color and appearance of *vanilla cream candy* ; others are set in
sulphate of lime, in the form of a rose; and others still roll out from the base, in forms resembling the ornaments on the capitol of a Corin-
thian column.   (You see how I am driven for
analogies.)   Some of the incrustations are massive and splendid; others are as delicate as the
lily, or as fancy-work of shell or wax.   Think
of traversing an arched way like this for a mile
and a half, and all the wonders of the tales of
youth—"Arabian Nights," and all—seem tame,
compared with the living, growing reality.   Yes,
growing reality; for the process is going on be-

fore your eyes. Successive coats of these incrustations, have been perfected and crowded off by others; so that hundreds of tons of these gems lie at your feet, and are crushed as you pass, while the work of restoring the ornaments for nature's *boudoir*, is proceeding around you. Here and there, through the whole extent, you will find openings in the sides, into which you may thrust the person, and often stand erect in little grottoes, perfectly incrusted with a delicate white substance, reflecting the light from a thousand glittering points. All the way you might have heard us exclaiming, " Wonderful, wonderful! O, Lord, how manifold are thy works!" With general unity of form and appearance, there is considerable variety in " the Cabinet." The " *Snow-ball Room*," for example, is a section of the cave described above, some 200 feet in length, entirely different from the adjacent parts; its appearance being aptly indicated by its name. If a hundred rude school boys had but an hour before completed their day's sport, by throwing a thousand snow-balls against the roof, while an equal number were scattered about the floor, and all petrified, it would have

8

presented precisely such a scene as you witness in this room of nature's frolics. So far as I know, these "snow-balls are a perfect anomaly among all the strange forms of crystalization. It is the result, I presume, of an unusual combination of the sulphates of lime and magnesia, with a carbonate of the former. We found here and elsewhere in the Cabinet, fine specimens of the sulphate of Magnesia, (or Epsom salts,) a foot or two long, and three inches in thickness.

Leaving the quiet and beautiful "Cabinet," you come suddenly upon the "Rocky Mountains," furnishing a contrast so bold and striking, as almost to startle you. Clambering up the rough side some thirty feet, you pass close under the roof of the cavern you have left, and find before you an immense transverse cave, 100 feet or more from the ceiling to the floor, with a huge pile of rocks half filling the hither side—they were probably dashed from the roof in the great earthquake of 1811. Taking the left hand branch, you are soon brought to "Croghan's Hall," which is nine miles from the mouth, and is the farthest point explored in that direction. The "Hall" is 50 or 60 feet in diameter, and

perhaps, thirty-five feet high, of a semi-circular
form. Fronting you as you enter, are massive
stalactites, ten or fifteen feet in length, attached to
the rock, like sheets of ice, and of a brilliant color.
The rock projects near the floor, and then re-
cedes with a regular and graceful curve, or swell,
leaving a cavity of several feet in width between
it and the floor. At intervals, around this swell,
stalactites of various forms are suspended, and
behind the sheet of stalactites first described,
are numerous stalagmites, in fanciful forms. I
brought one away that resembles the horns
of the deer, being nearly translucent. In the
centre of this hall, a very large stalactite hangs
from the roof; and a corresponding stalagmite
rises from the floor, about three feet in height
and a foot in diameter, of an amber color, perfectly smooth and translucent, like the other formations. On the right, is a deep pit, down
which the water dashes from a cascade that
pours from the roof. Other avenues could most
likely be found by sounding the sides of the pit,
if any one had the courage to attempt the descent. We are far enough from *terra supra,*
and our dinner which we had left at the " Vine-

yard." We hastened back to the Rocky Mountains, and took the branch which we left at our right on emerging from the Cabinet .Pursuing the uneven path for some distance, we reached "Serena's Arbor," which was discovered but three months since, by our guide "Mat." The descent to the Arbor seemed so perilous, from the position of the loose rocks around, that several of the party would not venture. Those of us who scrambled down regarded this as the crowning object of interest. The "Arbor" is not more than twelve feet in diameter, and of about the same height, of a circular form; but is, of itself, floor, sides, roof, and ornaments, one perfect, seamless stalactite, of a beautiful hue, and exquisite workmanship. Folds or blades of stalactitic matter hang like drapery around the sides, reaching half way to the floor; and opposite the door, a canopy of stone projects, elegantly ornamented, as if it were the resting-place of a fairy bride. Every thing seemed fresh and new; indeed, the invisible architect has not quite finished this master-piece; for you can see the pure water, trickling down its tiny channels and perfecting the delicate points of some of the

stalactites.   Victoria, with all her splendor, has
not in Windsor Castle, so beautiful an apartment as " Serena's Arbor."

Such is the description of Cleveland's Avenue,
as given by this clerical gentleman. It is perfectly graphic, and corresponds with all the glow-
ing accounts I have read of this famous place.
Exquisitely beautiful and rare as are the formations in this avenue, it will soon be, I fear, like
the Grotto of Pensico — shorn of its beauties.
Many a little Miss, to decorate her centre table
or boudoir, and many a thoughtless dandy to
present a specimen to his lady fair, have broken
from the walls (regardless of the published rules
prohibiting it,) those lovely productions of the
Almighty, which required ages to perfect; thus
destroying in a moment the work of centuries.
These beautiful and gorgeous formations were
encrusted on the walls by the hands of our
Maker, and who so impious as to desecrate
them — to tear them from their place? there
they are, all lovely and beautiful, and there they
ought to remain, *untouched* by the hands of man,
for the admiration and wonder of all future ages.
If the comparatively small cave of Adelburg

8*

which belongs to the Emperor of Austria, be
placed for the preservation of its formations
under the protecting care of the goverment (as is
the case,) what ought not to be done to preserve
the mineralogical treasures, in this great Cave
of America, and especially in Cleveland's Cabinet, which are worth more than all the caves in
Europe, indeed of the world, so far as our knowledge of caverns extends.

Returning from Serena's Arbor, we passed
on our left the mouth of an avenue more than
three miles long, lofty and wide, and at its termination there is a hall, which in the opinion of
the guide is larger than any other in the Cave.
It is as yet without a name. Equidistant from
the commencement and the termination of Cleveland's Avenue, is a huge rock, nearly circular,
flat on the top and three feet high. This is the
"*dining table.*" More than one hundred persons
could be seated around this table; on it the
guide arranged our dinner, and we luxuriated on
"flesh and fowl" and "choice old sherry." Never
did a set of fellows enjoy dinner more than we
did ours. Our friend B. was perfectly at his

ease and happy; and, in the exuberance of his
spirits, proposed the following toast:

"Prosperity to the subterranean territory of Cimmeria; large enough, if
not populous enough, for admission into the Union as an independent
State."

We emptied our glasses and gave nine hearty
cheers in honor of the sentiment. A proposi-
tion was made to adjourn, but B. was not in
clined to locomotion, and opposed it with great
warmth, insisting that it was too soon to
move after such a dinner, and that a state of
rest was absolutely essential to healthy digestion.
We had much argument on the motion to adjourn; when our sagacious guide Stephen, with
a meaning look interposed, saying "we had as
well be going, for the river might take a rise and
shut us up here." "What!" exclaimed B. in utter
consternation, and with a start, literally bouncing
from his seat, cried aloud "Let's be off!" at the
same time suiting the action to the word. In a
second we were all in motion, and hurrying past
beautiful incrustations, through galleries long
and tortuous, down one hill and up another,
(poor B. puffing and blowing, and all the while
'xclaiming against the *terrible* length and rug-

gedness of the way,) we at last reached the Echo,
which we found to our great relief had *not risen*.
It seems, the guide had used this stratagem for our
own advantage, to break off our banquet, lest
it trenched too far upon the night. We were
too happy in having our fears relieved, to fall
out with him. On our homeward bound passage over the rivers, our admiration was rather
increased than diminished. The death-like
stillness! the awful silence! the wild grandeur
and sublimity of the scene, tranquilizing the
feeling and disposing to pensive musings and
quiet contemplation; on a sudden a pistol is
fired — a tremendous report ensues — its echoes
are heard reverberating from wall to wall, in
caves far away, like the low murmuring sound
of distant thunder — the spell of silence and deep
reverie is broken — we become roused and ani-
mated, and the mighty cavern resounds with
our song. We believe every one will, under
similar circumstances, experience this sudden
transition from pensive musings to joyous hilarity.
Leaving the rivers, we hastened onward to the
outlet to the upper world. Far ahead we per-
ceive the first *dawnings of day*, shining with

a silvery pallid hue on the walls, and increasing in brightness as we advance, until it bursts forth in all the golden rays and glorious effulgence of the setting sun. This *parting* scene is lovely and interesting. We bid adieu to the "Great Monarch of Caves." We here terminate our subterranean tour. Standing on the grassy terrace above, we inhale the cool, pure air, and take a last look at the "great Wonder of Wonders!" To all we would say "go and see — explore the greatest of the Almighty's subterranean works." No description can give you an idea of it — neither can inspection of other caves; it is "the Monarch of Caves! none that have ever been measured can at all compare with it, in extent, in grandeur, in wild, solemn, serene, unadorned majesty; it stands entirely alone. — "It has no brother; it has no brother."